Heavenwards

by

Mother Mary Loyola

edited by

Rev. Herbert Thurston, S.J.

2015

ST. AUGUSTINE ACADEMY PRESS

HOMER GLEN, ILLINOIS

This book is newly typeset based on the edition published in 1910 by P.J. Kenedy & Sons. All editing strictly limited to the correction of errors in the original text and minor clarifications in punctuation or phrasing. Any remaining oddities of spelling or phrasing are as found in the original.

Nihil Obstat
REMIGIUS LAFORT, S.T.L.
Censor

Imprimatur
✠JOHN M. FARLEY, D.D.,
Archbishop of New York

April 22, 1910.

This book was originally published in 1910 by Burns & Oates.
This edition ©2015 by St. Augustine Academy Press.
Editing by Larry and Lisa Bergman.

ISBN: 978-1-936639-31-1
Library of Congress Control Number: 2015943307

"Catholic literature, doctrinal and devotional, owes a great deal to Mother Mary Loyola. There is a certain wholesomeness, naturalness, geniality about her spirituality that at once wins a place in the Catholic heart for whatever she writes." --The Ecclesiastical Review, volume 58, January 1918

About Mother Mary Loyola:

Most Catholics today who have heard the name Mother Mary Loyola know her as the author of *The King of the Golden City*, which has enjoyed a resurgence in popularity in recent years. But few know that she wrote over two dozen works, and that she was once a household name among Catholics of her era. What made her unique among Catholic authors was her ability to draw in her listeners with story after story—and not just any stories, but ones that incorporated current events and brand new inventions of the time. Despite the fact that those events are no longer current, and those inventions no longer brand new, her books scintillate with the appeal of an active mind that could find a moral in the most unusual places. And while the printed word lacks the animated facial expressions and vocal inflections which reveal a gifted storyteller, hers convey her enthusiasm so capably that the reader can easily imagine sitting at the feet of this wise old nun.

About *Heavenwards*:

"It is our lot to journey to heaven backwards, so to speak, with our face to the enemy. It is not an easy journey. There is not a little danger that, while we drive off successfully many violent attacks, we may be brought to earth by obstacles that crop up in our path unseen....*Heavenwards* brings out for us many of these dangers, diagnoses them, and shows us a way out of the difficulty; it puts into words many a source of disquiet that we feel but cannot quite express....There is about it a certain air of cheerfulness and encouragement that is very helpful. We feel driven to strive after holiness, and to trust what is past to God's Providence." —The Tablet, October 1910

To learn more about Mother Mary Loyola, visit our website at
www.staugustineacademypress.com.

"And his countenance was as lightning, and his raiment as snow.
And for fear of him, the guards were struck with terror,
and became as dead men." (Mt 28:3-4)

TO

Mother Church

WHOSE OFFICE AND AIM
IS TO KEEP OUR HEARTS ABOVE
THE DANGERS, TRIALS, AND
ALLUREMENTS
OF THIS PASSING WORLD
AND WHOSE DAILY ADMONITION
FROM A THOUSAND ALTARS
IS EVER

"Sursum Corda!"

CONTENTS

	PREFACE	xi
I	LÆTATUS SUM	1
II	THE HEWING OF THE STONES	8
III	SECRETS I	11
IV	SECRETS II	17
V	OUR FATHER	25
VI	"COME TO ME ALL!"	27
VII	"I SEND MY ANGEL" I	32
VIII	"I SEND MY ANGEL" II	39
IX	THE BOOK OF LIFE	44
X	"CROOKED WAYS"	48
XI	MEDIOCRITY *versus* EXCELLENCE	54
XII	HAIL MARY	65
XIII	"US ALSO"	70
XIV	"WHO IS MY NEIGHBOUR?"	72
XV	HARD PRAYER	76
XVI	"WHO IS THIS?"	80
XVII	LEST WE FORGET	83

XVIII	GIVE US THIS DAY OUR DAILY BREAD	88
XIX	"ALL THY WAYS ARE PREPARED"	91
XX	"TOLLE LEGE!"	93
XXI	BEFORE CONFESSION	96
XXII	GOD WITH US	98
XXIII	EVENTIDE	102
XXIV	IN THE STORM	108
XXV	MY CREATOR	112
XXVI	"STIR UP THY MIGHT...STIR UP OUR HEARTS, O LORD"	116
XXVII	"GLORIOUS IN HOLINESS"	119
XXVIII	"THIS IS THE WILL OF GOD CONCERNING YOU"	122
XXIX	LOVE IN CHASTISEMENT	125
XXX	"OPEN TO ME"	129
XXXI	"THE SON OF MAN"	134
XXXII	"THESE THREE"	139
XXXIII	DETAILS	143
XXXIV	"WHAT WILT THOU THAT I DO FOR THEE?"	149
XXXV	"DOMINE NON SUM DIGNUS!"	154
XXXVI	"REASONABLE SERVICE"	157
XXXVII	TRUE LOVE	162
XXXVIII	"BE READY"	165
XXXIX	VISITS	170
XL	WILLFULNESS	175
XLI	THIRST	180
XLII	PLENTIFUL REDEMPTION	187
XLIII	"THE DAY OF OUR LORD JESUS CHRIST"	194

Contents

XLIV	St. Mary Magdalen	202
XLV	Trust	205
XLVI	Running	208
XLVII	"Lord, Teach Us To Pray"	210
XLVIII	Our Angel Guardian	212
XLIX	"The Serpent Deceived Me"	215
L	O Sacrum Convivium	220
LI	Patience	222
LII	Sursum Corda!	229

PREFACE

"EN," so Joubert wrote, just after the French Revolution, "have torn up the roads which led to Heaven and which all the world followed; now we have to make our own ladders." Whatever truth may have underlain these words at the beginning of the 19th century, they certainly have lost nothing of their point in the hundred years which have passed since they were first uttered. Never was there a period when young Catholics in their journey heavenward could count less upon public opinion and the force of good example to keep them in the right path. We may doubt if it has at any time been true that men were swept along in the crush and were carried to Heaven by their surroundings almost in spite of themselves. But if such days ever existed, they are with us no longer. Heaven is now for all of us more or less a matter of scaling ladders. The broad road has grown broader with every new discovery of science and in much the same proportion the narrow way has grown narrower. Every new facility of communication has filled modern life with greater restlessness and with the craving for fresh emotional excitement. Those who may read in such an old-fashioned work as Father Parsons' *Christian Directory* his impressive exposition of the text: "with desolation the world is laid desolate because no man thinketh in his heart," can hardly forbear to smile at the venerable writer's earnestness when they compare the distractions of modern life with the life of three centuries back. Nevertheless we have to save our souls in the surroundings in which God has placed us. Nothing is to be gained by looking only at the difficulties and discouragements. Things have not all altered for the worse, and to the credit side of the account in the work of salvation as it presents itself to the modern Christian, must surely be set such helps as Mother Mary Loyola offers to her thousands of readers in books like the present.

What seems specially recommendable in these pages is the cheerful encouragement offered to all to look steadily forward to the goal of human life. The words *Sursum corda* (Lift up your hearts) which embody the spirit of so many of these chapters, strike, as all will recognise, a note of consolation and of joy. The thought of "Home" brings peace to the soul, while at the same time it should be enough to call forth our best energies. Thus while Mother Loyola teaches us how to find "ladders" to scale Heaven, she lets us see that the most arduous part of the task lies in the simple resolution to fix our eyes steadily upon the welcome that awaits us. Once we do this, the fatigue of the road is lightened, death loses its terrors, the world has little power to distract, and we shall enjoy even here below some share of the happiness which is promised us in paradise.

> Uni trinoque Domino
> Sit sempiterna gloria
> Qui vitam sine termino
> Nobis donet in patria.

HERBERT THURSTON, S. J.

Laetatus sum
in his quae dicta
sunt mihi:
In domum
Domini ibimus.

I

LÆTATUS SUM

"I rejoiced in what hath been told me, we shall go into the House of the Lord." (Ps. 121:1.)

TRULY a cause for rejoicing—the good news fresh every day, brought home to me at my morning prayer; in Mass and Holy Communion; whenever I say: "Our Father who art in Heaven"; whenever I hear, "Life everlasting," "*Sursum corda*," "We are to go into the House of the Lord."

We—not I alone. The joy is multiplied because to all the dear human race the invitation has gone out, to every redeemed soul the gates are thrown open.

Yet there are some who find in this universality of Redemption, this desire of the Creator to draw to Himself every one of His creatures, an argument against His singular love for them in particular.

"Our Lord indeed died for me on the Cross," they say, "but it was not for me alone. He died for all. I am only one among the redeemed. I am not singled out for individual notice and love in the crowd now going up to the House of the Lord."

What! not singled out, not specially considered, because all you hold dearest, all in any way connected with you are included in the invitation! Would this, then, be more acceptable to you if they were excluded? Does the peasant maiden whom the King calls to share His throne, deem herself less loved because all her kinsfolk are summoned with her to Court? Moses and St. Paul, those lovers of their people, went so far as to disclaim eternal happiness for themselves if their brethren might not share it. Let us at least own with joy and thankfulness that the delights of the House of the Lord are multiplied to us beyond measure because of the dear familiar faces we shall see lit up with its glory and its bliss.

And shall we grudge this cause for rejoicing to the rest of the elect, and not rather thank God that the joy of each is reflected as in dazzling mirrors on every side?

> ...I saw
> A hundred little spheres, that fairer grew
> By interchange of splendour.[1]

In that Land of perfect charity there is no solitary grandeur, no unshared joy. The days of *"meum et tuum"* are past. It is the co-heirship of that glorious heritage that makes the happiness of Heaven. "I saw a great multitude which no man could number, of all nations, and tribes, and peoples, and tongues, standing before the throne and in sight of the Lamb, clothed with white robes, and palms in their hands. And they cried with a loud voice saying: *Salvation to our God who sitteth upon the throne, and to the*

---

1   *Paradise.* Canto XXII. Dante. Translation of H. F. Cary, M. A.

Lamb. And all the Angels stood round about the throne, and the ancients and the four living creatures, and they fell down before the throne and adored God, saying: *Amen. Benediction, and glory, and wisdom, and thanksgiving, honour, and power, and strength to our God for ever and ever. Amen....*

And a voice came out from the throne saying: *Give praise to our God, all ye His servants, and you that fear Him, little and great.* And I heard as it were the voice of a great multitude, and as the voice of many waters, and as the voice of great thunders saying: *Alleluia; for the Lord our God the Almighty hath reigned."*

In this great chorus of praise in which Angels and men join in alternate choirs, we notice—what it is so useful to note in these days of ours—the self-annihilation of the worship before the Throne; the pride and triumph in their God; the glory of being His servants; the words "our God," again and again repeated by that exulting family of His children, the elder creation and the younger, before His Face. It is a common joy, a family joy, increased by every addition to the number of the Blessed, by the rapture and enthusiasm of each, by the special note of thanksgiving, the personal motives for glory and praise to God, brought by each.

We shall not rejoice that we are singularly beloved to the exclusion of others, but rather that we are accounted worthy to be one of that multitude whom no man can number standing before the Throne and in sight of the Lamb.

If we find selfishness cramping our hearts, let us go and sit down humbly at a pagan's feet and learn there

> ...that sympathy with Adam's race
> Which in each brother's history reads its own.[1]

"I am a man," said Plato, "everything human interests me." Or let us beg of God a share in His gift to Solomon: "And God gave to Solomon largeness of heart as the sand that is on the seashore."[2] Better still, let us beg of the Sacred Heart, so often close to our own, that It would widen ours till there is room there for every one of our brethren—that is, for every human soul.

We are not forbidden to crave a special place in the Mind of God and in the Sacred Heart of Jesus. When we meet our Lord at Judgment, and He unfolds to us His eternal designs over us and His dealings with us all life through, we shall be overwhelmed with joyful confusion at the sight of His singular love for us, at the almost incredible way in which our individual advantage has been studied, so to say, in the events that went on around us. But we have to bear in mind, that God's fatherly care is not less singular to each because it embraces all. Unlike our miserable little stream, which decreases in volume as it is divided, His love like the ocean overwhelms all, suffices for all, and is unspent, undiminished still.

And so I rejoice that *we*—all God's children united to Him by sanctifying grace, and the numbers, estranged from Him just now, but to be His again before the end, and for all eternity—are journeying to the House of the Lord.

1   *Verses on Various Occasions*, p. 129. Cardinal Newman.
2   3 Kings 4:29.

Two things are to be noted here—the House, and the approach to it. This, because the House stands high, is an ascent all the way, not always steep, not always painful, at times even pleasant, yet, owing to our slothful and untrained ways, our fickleness and love of ease, hard to most of us, perseverance on it to the end, to all of us. But there is encouragement in the very hardness. It shows we are on the right road, "the strait way that leadeth to life"[1] —and that is everything.

We shall go to the House—there must be effort, there must be progress. Yet we must not lose heart, as if advance to be real must be always patent. We advance if we make effort, if we persevere. We advance if we pray—coldly, it may be and with difficulty, yet regularly. We advance if we rise quickly after a fall; if we go frequently and with at least sufficient preparation to the fountains of grace, the Sacraments; if we keep up our heads and our hope through all the vicissitudes of the road, and the perplexing nature, at times, of God's dealings with us.

To the House of the Lord—"the place where Thy glory dwelleth."[2] What must it be in magnificence and in beauty! We are so accustomed to see our God contenting Himself for our sakes with all that is meanest in His creation, that we think but little of the splendour of the Heavenly Court. There are no images by which we can picture it: the fairest scenes of this fair world, heightened beyond the wildest flight of imagination, are comparisons too base to serve us. The words of Scripture, as might be expected, set us on the right track, but as human words, they, too, are utterly

1   Matthew 7:14.   2   Ps. 25:8.

inadequate to describe realities for which earth furnishes no counterpart. Where St. Paul fails, who shall hope to succeed? Caught up to the third heaven, he might have been expected to tell us something of its glory and its bliss. Yet he can only deal in negatives: "Eye hath not seen nor ear heard, nor hath it entered into the heart of man to conceive what God hath prepared for them that love Him."[1]

"Blessed are they who dwell in Thy House, O Lord, they shall praise Thee for ever and ever."[2] Our place there is being prepared by our own hands here and now. It is a part of God's tender plan for us that we should have the stimulus and satisfaction of carving out our own fortune, and at every moment of our probation here, by the humdrum work of each day, by every circumstance of joy or trial, be able to enrich our habitation for eternity.

"In my Father's House there are many mansions."[3] "The small and great are there."[4] We may rank with either; the choice is ours now, but time is passing fast, the night is at hand in which no man can work; if we want to lay up treasure in Heaven, there is no room for delay.

Majesty and familiarity we look upon as incompatible. When the Queen of Saba saw the house which Solomon had built, "she had no longer any spirit in her."[5] Not so will it be in the House of the Lord. Our Father's House is not glorious only but homely; we shall not be overpowered with splendour, but overwhelmed with welcomes and with love. There the deepest trembling worship will be no hindrance to a nearness of approach, a ravishing union

---

1 1 Cor. 2:9.　　2 Ps. 83:5.　　3 John 14:2.
4 Job 3:19.　　5 3 Kings 10:5.

with Him which throughout eternity will be ever fresh wonder and delight.

And this is in store for every one of us! As we set our feet each morning on our daily path, will not the brightness streaming down from our Home gild the stones and rough places of the way? Shall we not rejoice in the very weariness of each day's journey which brings us nearer to the end?

And will not the heartsinking that comes to us all at times make us mindful of our fellow travellers on the same road? Many of them have a harder lot than our own, carry heavier burdens, feel more the hardships and weariness of the way. God has placed us by their side to cheer and help them.

Others there are who have missed their road and are painfully seeking it. Others again have wilfully left the path and must regain it before nightfall. And then there are those whose night has come wherein no man can work. They have Home in sight and are sure of entrance there. But unless our charity succours them in their helpless suffering, they will be long shut out from its peace and joy. All these are with us *in via*, and all call upon us for the sympathy and assistance which fellow travellers have a right to claim. We are all children of the same Father, all redeemed at the same price, all called to the same eternal reward in our Heavenly Home, "the House of the Lord."

II

THE HEWING OF THE STONES

"And the house, when it was in building, was built of stones hewed and made ready, so that there was neither hammer nor axe nor any tool of iron heard in the house when it was in building." (3 Kings 6:7.)

HAT a sight it must have been—that rising of Solomon's glorious Temple day after day, and year after year, the builders at their silent work receiving the stones made ready to their hands and laying them in place! What a scene again the far-off mountains where with noise and labour the eighty thousand masons hewed and squared the stones!

The Church sees in all this a figure of the Jerusalem now building like a city[1] and of the preparation of the "living stones"[2] for their heavenly resting place.

> ....whereas on earth
> Temples and palaces are formed of parts
> Costly and rare, but all material,
> So in the world of spirits nought is found,
> To mould withal, and form into a whole,
> But what is immaterial; and thus
> The smallest portions of this edifice,

---

1   Ps. 121:3.   2   1 Peter 2:5.

Cornice or frieze, or balustrade, or stair,
The very pavement is made up of life—
Of holy, blessed, and immortal beings,
Who hymn their Maker's praise continually.[1]

Meanwhile the fashioning of the living stones is arduous work both for hewers and hewed. The more eminent the position to be occupied, the more careful is the preparation required, but for no part of the building is rough material accepted. "The king commanded that they should bring great stones, costly stones for the foundations, and should square them."[2]

Where and how are the living stones squared?

Here in this world, far away from the peace of the Heavenly City, and by means of the labours and trials of life. Each of these from the greatest to the least has its appointed task—to hew or to polish, not ruthlessly, nor recklessly, but in appointed measure, and to a definite end. There are the agonising pangs which do their work swiftly—separations, disillusions, failure, sharp suffering, physical and mental. And there is the constant chiselling of daily frets and worries, anxieties, and difficulties, less severe taken singly, but more trying by reason of the perpetual chafing, and the monotony of the pain. The stones are brought together at times in a contact too close to be pleasant. They rub up against each other, grate and jar upon one another, sometimes with sudden collision, sometimes with persistent friction. Very disagreeable, no doubt; very trying, but that is just how the corners get

---

1   *The Dream of Gerontius*, Cardinal Newman.
2   3 Kings 5:17.

rounded off and the polishing is done. We have to look to the end of the process, and think less of present labour and pain than of rest and reward everlasting.

Besides faith and hope, we have the counsel of common sense and every day philosophy to help us here. The world is a big quarry in which there is no escaping the strokes of misfortune. Experience shows that blows fall heaviest on those who seek to avert them, and that in the long run it is the impatient and the rebellious who suffer most, whereas patience under the hand of God, after the example of Christ and His Saints, not only satisfies for sin, and wins everlasting reward, but so assuages sorrow, that the sting and the bitterness of the trial are alleviated beyond all expectation, and borne not with resignation only, but with peace and joy.

Every motive, then, urges us to accept readily and even thankfully the conditions of our short life here. We cannot alter them, and unless we have let our hearts become warped by selfishness, we shall own that He who made us and made us for happiness, best knows the way that leads thereto, and that our wisdom and our welfare here and hereafter consist in leaving ourselves trustfully in His hands.

III

SECRETS

I

HERE has been a fascination about them from the beginning, due to the charm which attaches to mystery and the incentive they furnish to curiosity. It was this made Eve stop before the tree of the knowledge of good and evil, and wonder why the fruit that looked so fair and harmless was forbidden: which led her to listen to the tempter, and be brought, first to inquire into the reason of God's command, next to question His veracity, then to desire the knowledge of evil, and finally, to risk everything here and hereafter so she might penetrate behind the veil and assure herself by experience of what lay hidden there.

It almost looks as if those two in Paradise held, that because God had given them so much, He had wronged them by withholding anything, and by imposing an arbitrary command respecting one particular tree. Unless we suppose in them something of this petulance of spoiled children, it seems inconceivable that with the reverence for

Him in which their souls must have been steeped by their vast knowledge of His works and their close intercourse with Him, they should have dared to measure their strength with His, and provoke Him to the execution of that—to them mysterious threat—"you shall die the death."

The more we think of it, the more inexplicable appears the attitude of mind which led them to question His rights over them and all He had given them. Yet is not this what men have done ever since the first "Why?" was heard in Eden; what they are doing with more and more effrontery every day; what we ourselves do, times without number, in practice? We chafe under "the obedience of faith"[1] and the restraints of the Commandments; we want reasons for God's commands; we grudge Him His secrets; we are fretful with the uncertainties of the future and the obscurity which shrouds life beyond the grave.

Why is this? How comes it that we are so impatient and exacting, so unmindful of our position as creatures, that truth and justice—the foundation of all our relations with our fellow men—are forgotten in our dealings with Him who planted their instincts in our hearts?

We do not thus treat one another. Every man may screen off from his neighbour, nay, even from his nearest and dearest, not only the more intimate workings of his mind and heart, but as much of his plans and circumstances as he thinks proper to conceal. No one questions this right; on the contrary, to worm his secret from him or to discover it by treachery, is held to be the most flagrant injustice. We value the confidence our

---

1   Rom. 16:26.

friend shows us by letting us into his secrets precisely because this act is a spontaneous concession on his part. We take what he gives and, beyond this limit, respect his silence.

But this law of ordinary propriety does not hold good when there is question of the Incomprehensible God. What they cannot understand, too many either resent or deny. That He should have secrets, impenetrable to them, is intolerable; that He should require the subjection of their intellect to mysteries they cannot fathom, and the obedience of their will to laws that impose restraint on deed and word and thought, is an outrage on their reason and their liberty. But is it wonderful that the "God of the heavens and Lord of the whole creation"[1], "who has made all things that are under the cope of heaven"[2], should have secrets incommunicable to *us?* "The works of the Highest are glorious, and secret, and hidden."[3] "Who shall search out His glorious acts?"[4] "What we can know is as a spark,"[5] "for we have seen but a few of His works"[6]. "We shall say much and yet shall want words; but the sum of our words is, He is all."[7]

Society visits with heavy penalties those who forget their place in it, and the higher the ground trespassed on, the more heinous is the offence. If amongst men, who after all are equal as to essentials, pretence is so insufferable, how must the airs we give ourselves in His Presence appear in the sight of the Lord of heaven and earth!

---

1   Judith 9:17.   2   Esther 13:10.   3   Ecclus. 11:4.
4   Ecclus. 18:3.   5   Ecclus. 42:23.   6   Ecclus. 43:36.
7   Ecclus. 43:29.

We resent the inevitable. We expect the Incomprehensible to be easily understood, or we will not believe. "How can these things be?" Nicodemus asked. "Art thou a master in Israel and knowest not these things?" was our Lord's reply. "If I have spoken to you earthly things and you believe not, how shall you believe if I shall speak to you heavenly things?" The ABC was beyond the master in Israel; how could he attain to the comprehension of the sublimest truth!

Impossibilities are not asked of us. We are required to believe on the word of God, not to understand. And this should not be difficult. For if God by His very nature is incomprehensible, He is also the very Truth. What He reveals we can never fully understand, but reason itself tells us we can render it fullest belief. "It is not necessary for thee to see with thy eyes those things which are hid."[1] Nor is it desirable. Better to lie on our face and adore in silence than to peer curiously into what is beyond and above us. It is not so much that our weak eyes want light, as that the light is too strong for them: "He that is a searcher of majesty shall be oppressed by glory."[2] Better to trust the love that with the same hand gives and withholds, than to pine for knowledge that we are not ready for yet. "What I do thou knowest not now but thou shalt know hereafter."[3] "I have yet many things to say to you but you cannot bear them now."[4]

Not only are there depths in the Divine counsels that we could not fathom, but sights we could not bear, and

---

1   Ecclus. 3:23.   2   Prov. 25:27.   3   John 13:7.
4   John 16:12.

calls for generosity which with our present grace we could not meet.

> Did we but see,
> When life first open'd, how our journey lay
> Between its earliest and its closing day,
> Or view ourselves as we one time shall be
> Who strive for the high prize, such sight would break
> The youthful spirit, though bold for Jesu's sake.[1]

It is a merciful Providence that hides these things from us. We misread continually what we do see, or think we see—injustice and oppression carrying all before them, meek virtue unrequited and trodden under foot; the prosperous sated with the good things of life, the patience of the poor strained beyond endurance; the good cause failing on a thousand fields, evil unchecked and triumphant everywhere. We are puzzled and troubled by the strange littlenesses and frailty of the good, the success of the wicked, the scandals in holy places, the defeat of high endeavour, the fascination of the broad way, the power of temptation, the unaccountable patience and predilections of God, the sufferings of the innocent and the helpless.

Life is full of problems for us, but many of them are only such from our faltering faith in the Wisdom and Love and Sovereignty of God. We credit a general with ability to carry through a well-laid plan; we trust the workman with the frail vessel he commits to the furnace. But that the Almighty and the All-wise should be able to bring triumphantly through conflicting elements His own eternal designs—this is a trial to our faith!

---

1   *Our Future. Verses on Various Occasions.*   Cardinal Newman.

The thought of the Sovereignty of God is very helpful when we come back weary and perplexed from an outlook on men and things, and find no answer to the questions that disturb us:

"Thou art just, O Lord, and Thy judgment is right."[1]

"The judgments of the Lord are true, justified in themselves."[2]

"Is it not lawful for me to do what I will?"[3]

"And he said: *I believe, Lord,* and falling down he adored Him."[4]

---

1 Ps. 118:137.   2 Ps. 18:10.   3 Matthew 20:15.
4 John 9:38.

I V

SECRETS

II

GOD has His secrets—and we have ours. And, as mutual love demands, we exchange them. He tells us His as far as it is good for us to know them; we pour ours day and night into His willing ear.

Everyone knows how confidence in this shape wins the heart. It is one of the surest ways of detecting a budding friendship. Some one tells us his secret, and forthwith, from being careless listeners, we find ourselves transformed into eager admirers or sympathisers, ready to champion against all comers the cause of our new client. Such is the instantaneous response that the trust of another wakes in the human heart.

And not there only but in the Heart of God Himself. He loves our trust and therefore He loves to hear our secrets. It is no objection to say that He knows them already. He counts as unknown what He does not hear from ourselves. "What are these discourses which you hold one with another as you walk, and are sad?" Did He

not know? Did He need the long story of the two disciples
on the road to Emmaus to acquaint Him with the event of
the Friday? No, but He loved to have them confide it all
to Him. Their hearts needed the unburdening, and as a
perfect listener He let them tell out all their trouble, as if for
the first time He had heard of the mighty Prophet and His
condemnation and death. What a relief that outpouring to
Him must have been!

"Yes," we say perhaps, "for there was the near Presence
and the Voice and the virtue that went forth from Him to
work the change and make their hearts burn within them.
All this is wanting to us."

Not all; the Presence and the virtue, all but the
outward Form and the Voice, we too may have. We must
not be petulant with God, nor dictate conditions to Him,
nor let His marvellous condescension make us forget our
place. We must not act like fretful children who push
from them a costly gift because it is not the toy on which
they have set their hearts. If we would think a little more
of the amazing way in which He stoops to us, and allows
us intercourse with Himself, there would be no room
for repining because we have not here and now what is
reserved for us in Heaven.

Nor must we object that God knows what we want
before we ask. *We* do not know what *He* wants. He has
designs over us that we could never have guessed, graces
He intends to give us for ourselves and for others, and it
is through prayer that these graces are given. The object of
prayer is not only, as we are too apt to think, to get from
God all we can, but to place ourselves at His disposal that

He may do His Will in us and get from us the best service He can.

There are difficulties in this intercourse, no doubt, but not greater than those which attend our confidences to one another. How often it may happen that the disclosure of our secret to a friend leaves us more troubled than before. We spoke in an unguarded moment and regret our confidence now; or we question his prudence and so fear for its safety; or we were under the influence of strong feeling which so affected our representation of the affair as to oblige us to distrust the counsel given. Or again, the complications of the situation were not grasped, the advice was wide of the mark and we are in a worse plight than before. Even when our trouble is understood, and meets with the kindest sympathy, how often the power to help is wanting! How often, too, it is we ourselves who have been wide of the mark; *we* could not grasp our trouble which, like some volatile spirit, escapes when we want to analyse it. How should another deal satisfactorily with what we cannot bring to light!

Now, all this has no place in our relations with God. "No thought escapeth Him, and no word can hide itself from Him."[1] "Say not: I shall be hidden from God"... for "every heart is understood by Him."[2] "He seeth from eternity to eternity and there is nothing wonderful before Him."[3] The good and the bad in us He knows: "My offences are not hidden from Thee," says David[4]; and on the other hand He Himself says: "I know thy works, and

---

1 Ecclus. 42:20. 2 Ecclus. 16:16, 20. 3 Ecclus. 39:25.
4 Ps. 68:6.

thy faith and thy charity, and thy patience."[1]

When we speak to our Father who seeth in secret[2] we speak to Him who sees the whole trouble from beginning to end *as it is*, with perfect clearness of detail, through all its intricacies, with all its influences and consequences for ourselves and for others. We have not to choose our words carefully lest we be misunderstood, or fear the effects of overwrought fancy, or the danger of harming others. With what astounding boldness Job speaks out the anguish of his soul before God: "I will speak to the Almighty, and I desire to reason with God."[3]

"Am I a sea or a whale that Thou hast enclosed me in a prison?...Thou wilt frighten me with dreams and terrify me with visions....I have done with hope...spare me for my days are nothing....How long wilt Thou not spare me... what shall I do to Thee, O keeper of men? Why hast Thou set me opposite to Thee and I am become burdensome to myself? Why dost Thou not remove my sin?"[4]

"Tell me why Thou judgest me so. Doth it seem good to Thee that Thou shouldst calumniate me and oppress me the work of Thy hands?"[5]

His "troublesome comforters," scandalised at language which seemed to them intemperate, not to say blasphemous, took upon themselves to champion God Almighty and to reprove with indignant zeal His afflicted servant. Job replies meekly: "Indeed I know it is so...what am I that I should answer Him and have words with Him?[6] What can I answer who have spoken inconsiderately? I will lay my

---

1 Apoc. 2:19.   2 Matthew 6:4.   3 Job 13:3.
4 Job 7:12-21.   5 Job 10:2-3.   6 Job 9:2, 14.

hand upon my mouth.[1] I have spoken unwisely and things that above measure exceed my knowledge...Therefore I reprehend myself and do penance in dust and ashes."[2]

Did God reprehend him?

And the Lord said to Eliphaz the Themanite: "My wrath is kindled against thee and against thy two friends, because you have not spoken the thing that is right before Me, as My servant Job hath....Go to My servant Job and offer for yourselves a holocaust: and My servant Job shall pray for you: his face I will accept, that folly be not imputed to you: for you have not spoken right things before Me as My servant Job hath....And the Lord gave Job twice as much as he had before...and the Lord blessed the latter end of Job more than his beginning."[3]

We should read this marvellous history to know the lengths to which expostulation with God may go, and be consistent with humility, reverence and absolute trust; the condescension of God in justifying His dealings with us; the zeal with which He takes upon Himself the defence of His servants; His delight in their fidelity under trial; and the joy with which He hastens to praise and reward when the hour for both has come. Like St. Paul later, Job knew in whom he had believed, and he was not afraid that his bold words would draw upon him rebuke and punishment.

"For behold my Witness is in Heaven, and He that knoweth my conscience is on high."[4] "Although He should kill me I will trust in Him...and He shall be my Saviour."[5]

---

1   Job 39:34.   2   Job 42:3, 6.   3   Job 42:7-8, 10, 12.
4   Job 16:20.   5   Job 13:15.

"Secret things to the Lord our God,"[1] is the admonition of Scripture. Have we no secret things to confide to Him? No discontent perhaps, with a life of aimless drifting, a life of which self is the beginning and the end? Is there no longing at times for "a more excellent way,"[2] a more strenuous service of God, a more honest return to Him for all He has spent on us? Have we no secret fears for ourselves or for those we love, of which to tell Him?

Some of us take as our motto: "My secret to myself, my secret to myself,"[3] and seek counsel of none in time of need. This is unwise, for Scripture says: "Take wise counsel."[4] "Say not: I am sufficient for myself."[5] Some, going to the other extreme, so far forget the advice of the Holy Spirit: "Let one of a thousand be thy counsellor,"[6] that they seek a thousand counsellors in every difficulty, and what is worse, make free not with their own secrets only but with those of others. In both these classes there is indiscretion. And both, perhaps, neglect the recommendation: "Secret things to the Lord our God."

If we would train ourselves to take to Him all that concerns us—desires, responsibilities, plans, perplexities, hopes, and fears, and disappointments, failure and success, our falls and our victories, our defects natural and acquired; how a temptation teases us, or the sense of sin or distance from God weighs upon us; how the illness of a friend is going badly, or indiscriminate reading is harming one we love—talking all this over with Him simply and trustfully as with our best and most trusty friend, we should soon

1 Deut. 29:29.   2 1 Cor. 12:31.   3 Isaias 24:16.
4 Ecclus. 6:24.   5 Ecclus. 11:26.   6 Ecclus. 6:6.

find the reward of our confidence in the union with Him that intercourse such as this brings about, a union which does not end with our time of prayer but is a resource all day long and all life through. We should find that we have in Him what we want in ourselves—light, and strength, and the peace which passeth all understanding.

Talking over our concerns as with a friend, we have said, but indeed this is saying too little, for "I will not level God with man."[1] The most intimate converse that friendship can inspire is but a feeble shadow of what our intercourse with God may be, of the absolute freedom and trust with which, by a single word, or without word at all, we may lay open our souls before Him with whom we have relations unspeakably closer and more tender than any here on earth.

We call Him Father, Brother, Friend. We should call Him also Mother, Sister, Bridegroom, Lover. All these—and infinitely more than earth's tenderest names imply—He is to us, and therefore He claims as His right the privilege of all these sweet relations—to hear all about us from ourselves. If He says to us: "Treat thy cause with thy friend,"[2] much more does He expect to hear that cause Himself. "Come to Me all you who labour,"[3] is His invitation to us every one. The Incarnation and the Eucharist are but the expression of His desire to be with us and intimately united with us, a desire so vehement that it breaks through all barriers, flings aside the laws of Nature, and creates for itself a whole world of miracle and mystery, bewildering and overpowering to all but Faith.

---

1   Job 32:21.   2   Prov. 25:9.   3   Matthew 11:28.

Oh what we lose by ignoring Love like this! We scorn its advances and go our way, one to his farm, another to his merchandise, never dreaming of the blessings that would have overflowed even upon our interests of this world had we treated of them first with our Friend.

It must be allowed that this constant and trustful recourse to God, like all other good habits, takes time to form. At first the effort will be irksome; our restless nature will want the sights and sounds of response that reward the confidences of friends. We must have patience and persevere. Response will come, more direct, more surprising, more helpful by far than any friendship of this world could bring. "Wait a little while," says Job[1], and Judith: "Let us humbly wait for His consolation"[2], "for they shall not be confounded that wait for Him."[3]

> I see that thou believest these things
> Because I tell them, but discern'st not how;
> So that thy knowledge waits not on thy faith:
> As one who knows the name of thing by rote,
> But is a stranger to its properties,
> Till other's tongue reveal them. Fervent love
> And lively hope with violence assail
> The kingdom of the heavens and overcome
> The will of the Most High; not in such sort
> As man prevails o'er man; but conquers it
> Because 'tis willing to be conquer'd; still,
> Though conquer'd, by its mercy, conquering.[4]

---

1 Job 6:19.   2   Judith 8:20.   3   Isaias 49:23.
4 *Paradise.* Canto XX. Dante

V

OUR FATHER

"Is not He thy Father?" (Deut. 32:6.)

HE revelation of Himself given to us in this name, explains every other revelation and, in a sense, demands every other. If the Eternal God is our Father, what may we not expect? The Incarnation, the Redemption, the Eucharist, the Church with its infallible guidance, the forgiveness of sins, the everlasting inheritance—all flow from the blessed truth that we are children of God, and "most dear children."[1]

To seek us when we had strayed from Him, the Eternal Son must come on earth. His Blood is not too great a price to pay for our ransom; His whole Humanity and Divinity are not too stupendous a food for our daily nourishment. The Providence of our Heavenly Father must extend to every detail of our lives, His Wisdom make every circumstance, every alternation of joy and sorrow turn to our good, if we will only correspond with His designs.

When we turn our back upon our Father's Home, and, shaking off the restraint of His Presence, waste in self-indulgence the precious gifts He had entrusted to us, He

---

1   Ephes. 5:1.

does not give us up, nor transfer His love elsewhere, but follows us with His pity and compassion, and patiently waits for our return. He never tires of us. Our defects and shortcomings, the selfishness, changeableness, and inconsistency which disconcert at times even our best friends, do not disgust Him. He can bear to know us just as we are—and love us still.

We use His gifts against Him, and He presses new ones upon us; we are shamelessly shabby with Him, and, as if He had not noticed it, He treats us in return with the most lavish generosity. He makes much of any little bit of service we do Him, is really pleased with it and repays it by a return altogether out of proportion to it. Let us put together all we have ever heard or seen of the tenderness and compassion of an earthly father, heighten it by all we can imagine of indulgence and forgiveness and solicitude, and we have not yet the faintest shadow of the love of our Father Who is in Heaven. Like an earthly father, He studies our character and tastes and needs. How often has sudden relief in pain of body or mind, or a startling answer to prayer, or a joyful surprise He has prepared for us, brought tears to our eyes! If it has been thus during our time of schooling here, what will it be when we are at Home!

O my Heavenly Father, let me keep close to Thy side; let me cling fast to Thy hand all the days of my life on earth. Let me worship Thee with profoundest adoration, surrender myself to Thee with unquestioning trust, and love Thee with all the filial affection of Thy most loving children, that so I may make what return I am able for letting me—nay, commanding me—to call Thee "Father."

V I

"COME TO ME ALL!"

IF we put into one scale the warnings of Scripture which might deter us from Holy Communion, and in the other the loving words that invite us to our Lord's Table, we shall see how surprisingly the last outweigh the first.

There is, it is true, His condemnation of the guest who came unprepared to the marriage feast; there are St. Paul's terrific words against those who eat this Bread unworthily. But who shall count the words and ways by which our Lord invites us to himself!

"Come to Me all you who labour."[1] "I am come not to call the just but sinners."[2] "If anyone thirst, let him come to Me."[3] "Suffer the little children to come to Me."[4] "All that the Father giveth Me shall come to Me and him that cometh to Me I will not cast out."[5] "I am the bread of life, he that cometh to Me shall not hunger....I am the living bread which came down from heaven. If any man eat of this bread he shall live for ever....Except you eat the flesh of the

| 1 Matthew 11:28. | 2 Mark 2:17. | 3 John 7:37. |
| 4 Mark 10:14. | 5 John 6:37. | |

Son of Man, and drink His blood, you shall not have life in you. He that eateth My flesh and drinketh My blood hath everlasting life and I will raise him up in the last day.... He that eateth My flesh and drinketh My blood abideth in Me and I in him. As I live by the Father, so he that eateth Me the same also shall live by Me."[1] "You will not come to Me that you may have life."[2] "If any man open to Me the door, I will come to him and will sup with him and he with Me."[3]

Invitations, threats, entreaties, promises—all these He uses, after the fashion of love, to bring about His union with us, to convince us that His "delights are to be with the children of men."[4] Let us think over three of these promises.

(1) *He that eateth My flesh and drinketh My blood abideth in Me and I in Him.* Ponder the amazing union implied in this mutual indwelling, like the ocean in the sponge and the sponge in the ocean.

Abideth—for it is not a passing visit that leaves no trace. This is true even of reception at long intervals. But much more in the case of frequent, and beyond our power to express in daily Communion, does Christ abide with and in the soul, the Sacramental Presence establishing a union that subsists by its fragrance and by its fruits after the precious time of thanksgiving is past, to vivify every action of the day and be renewed with ever increasing efficacy on the morrow.

(2) *He that eateth Me the same also shall live by Me.* The body lives by its daily food, and its life will be vigorous

---

1　John 6:35, 51-58.　　2　John 5:40.　　3　Apoc. 3:20.
4　Prov. 8:31.

in proportion as its nourishment is good and generous. Our soul feeds—daily if it will—on the noblest Food God Himself can provide, a Food that repairs unceasingly the losses sustained in the spiritual conflict, by venial sin, by want of vigilance, by infidelity to grace, by the drag of the corruptible body on the soul. Like corporal nourishment, but in an incomparably higher manner, it builds up, invigorates, heals, refreshes, delights, wards off disease and death. Is any soul so weak as not to gain some strength from this Divine Food? Can any disease persistently resist this remedy? What more can Omnipotent Love do than give us—not Its help only, but Itself, by the undreamed-of device of becoming our Food, and in this way uniting us with the Source of all good! "I am come that they may have life and may have it more abundantly."[1]

Here we draw from the Saviour's fountains the courage we need in the battle of life; patience with others and with self; the brave humility that rises promptly after every fall; the right intention that sanctifies our words and works; the charity that seeks not its own and brightens life for all around it; perseverance in well-doing, in monotonous work, in that dry and seemingly unanswered prayer which is the great difficulty in the service of God. Here, from our union with Him, we learn little by little to "put on Christ,"[2] to see from His standpoint, to adopt His judgments of passing and eternal things, to take to heart His interests, to desire nearness to Him even at the cost of pain and shame. Thus we come to live by Him; thus His life within us shows itself in all manner of spiritual beauty and fruitfulness.

---

1   John 10:10.   2   Gal. 3:27.

(3) *He that eateth My flesh and drinketh My blood hath everlasting life, and I will raise him up in the last day."* This is the necessary consequence of a union with the Sacred Humanity, so close that earth can furnish no parallel with it. The soul of the worthy communicant has *now* eternal life in pledge and promise, and will be called hereafter to share in the life and glory of its Saviour. He who has not suffered His Holy One to see corruption, will raise up in glorious beauty those members of His which on earth have been so closely united to their Divine Head. "We know that when He shall appear we shall be like Him because we shall see Him as He is."[1]

Can we have further doubts as to His desire to see us often—daily, if possible—at His Table? Do we find the words of Scripture have been strained in their interpretation? Or is our hesitation in accepting and acting upon them due solely to the sense of our unworthiness?

Our Lord has removed this all-but-unsurmountable hindrance in a way perfectly marvellous. The Church, which in the past has been wary in her words and has only constrained her children under grievous penalty to Communion once in the year, has spoken her mind in our days with a clearness and an earnestness that should sweep away the last particle of honest difficulty from every mind. The Vicar of Christ has said what no theologian would have dared to say—that Christ our Lord desires to meet us one and all in the embrace of a daily Communion. The times grow more and more perilous as the end draws nearer; snares thicken; human respect

---

1   1 John 3:2

is more enslaving; the cares and pleasures of the world are more enthralling; the flesh is more exacting; the devil more wrathful, knowing that he has but a short time. We must have Christ with us if we are to overcome and persevere to the end. We must be drawn into His open arms—or driven into them.

And therefore Pius X has spoken—not indeed to constrain or lay any further injunction upon us, but to assure us so unmistakably of the desire of our God to be with us in frequent Communion, that henceforth the question is placed beyond the reach of doubt or even of discussion. No one may hinder us, no one may frighten us; the easiest of conditions are all we have to fulfil. Provided only we are free from conscious grievous sin, and that our intention is "right"—that is, provided we go from the motive of pleasing God, of gaining help in our spiritual needs, and the like—we may go to Him fearlessly, go to Him daily—and be welcome guests.

"O how good and sweet is Thy Spirit, O Lord!"[1]

---

1   Wisd. 12:1.

VII

"I SEND MY ANGEL"

I

*"Behold I will send My Angel who shall go before thee, and keep thee
in thy journey and bring thee into the place that I have prepared.
Take notice of him, and hear his voice, and do not think him one to be
contemned: for he will not forgive when thou hast sinned…But if thou
wilt hear his voice, and do all that I speak, I will be an enemy to thy
enemies, and will afflict them that afflict thee."* (Exod. 23:20-22.)

*"See that you despise not one of these little ones, for I say to you that
their Angels in Heaven always see the face of My Father
who is in Heaven."* (Matthew 18:10.)

AN easy method of prayer that combines mental
and vocal, is to take some familiar words
and dwell thoughtfully on them one by one,
extracting from each whatever of strength or fragrance or
sweetness we can get it to give out. The above passages on
the holy Angel Guardians lend themselves well to this kind
of prayer.

Behold!—A word used in Scripture to arrest the
attention or to express wonder at an announcement

to follow. Here God would have me consider intently a marvellous disposition of His Providence in my favour.

I send—This blessed spirit who is my constant companion has his commission from God Himself. As truly as the Angel Gabriel was sent to Mary, is my Angel sent to me. And it is not any Angel that is appointed as my guardian, but one selected out of all that innumerable host by the Wisdom of God and the Love of God, because of his special fitness for the guidance of my soul. The Holy Angels are not all alike, each has his own individuality as we have, his particular excellence and gifts by which he is known among the rest. And it is on account of these gifts that my Angel has been chosen by God for me. In consequence of this choice, God has given him a strong affection for my soul, with power to understand it and light for its direction. If I am wise I shall beg His Divine Majesty to give him more and more light about me; about my place in God's universal plan; the work I am called to do; my difficulties and dangers; the graces I need to be able to give to God the special service He condescends to ask of me; about my tendencies, my temptations, my duties. As to all these things I should pray God my Angel may know me thoroughly that he may keep me in safety.

My Angel—Thus does the Divine Goodness commend him to my reverence, my confidence, my love. He belongs to God. He has always been faithful to God. God loves him with a singular affection. Because of his nearness and dearness to God, I must reverence and love him.

Angel—What are these high and holy servants of His, one of whom God has appointed to serve me? They are beings made in His own image and likeness, and by reason of their purely spiritual nature they resemble Him more nearly than do any others among His creatures. In their gifts natural and supernatural they are immeasurably superior to us. "I saw another Angel come down from heaven having great power, and the earth was enlightened with his glory."[1] By the side of their knowledge of the natural world and their control over it, our knowledge and power dwindle into insignificance. Compared with their supernatural insight into the mysteries of God's dealings with His creatures, all our light is darkness indeed.

Yet these noble and glorious beings are our brethren, children of the same Father in Heaven, united by ties of the tenderest affection to those in whom they see their future companions. And one of them is deputed to be my constant attendant, guardian, teacher, defender, intercessor, brother, and friend.

Who shall go before thee—My Angel is truly my servant to prepare my way, to foresee occasions of danger and opportunities of merit, to provide me with the light, strength, succour, and consolation I need. Always at hand, always ready, he holds himself at my disposal every hour of the day and night. Where shall I find a servant so devoted, so joyous in his service as this prince of the Heavenly Court!

And keep thee in thy journey—If I could only bear in mind that I am a traveller, hurrying through this world which fascinates and engrosses me, to another world in which I am to live for ever! My path is beset with

---

1 Apoc. 18:1.

perils, from enemies deadly and cunning, from the false maxims, evil example, alluring pleasures that incite me to evil, from my own corrupt inclinations and passions more dangerous than all the rest. Amid all these obstacles my Angel is to keep me that my feet may not swerve from the narrow way, that I may not be overthrown by violence nor deceived by craft.

> ...to the guardian of my steps
> I turned me, like the child who always runs
> Thither for succour, where he trusteth most.[1]

And bring thee into the place that I have prepared.—Oh what joy for him and for me when he brings me in safety— to what? This God Himself cannot tell me; eye has not seen nor ear heard nor heart imagined what awaits me there. All He can tell me about it is that it is His preparation for me: "Come, blessed of My Father, possess the kingdom prepared for you from the foundation of the world."[2]

When we go to stay with a friend, we find our room telling in every direction of the mindfulness of one who knows us well—flowers, pictures, books, birds even—all our tastes have been consulted and provided for, nothing has been forgotten that may make us feel at home. So will it be in Heaven. He who knows what I need for satisfying to the full my capacity for happiness, for employing with full activity and delight every faculty of soul and body, has prepared this for me. All the Omnipotence and Wisdom of the Creator, all the tenderness of the most loving of fathers, all the insight and solicitude of a mother, all the love and providence of brother, benefactor, friend—all this has from

---

1　*Paradise*, Canto XXII. Dante.　　2　Matthew 25:34.

eternity gone to the preparation in the Heavenly mansions of my appointed place.

And now what charge does God give me as to the guide He has appointed to bring me thither?

Take notice of him—Could He ask less! Yet have I done this hitherto? What notice do I take of my Angel Keeper? How often do I give him a thought of gratitude for his faithful service and deliverance from dangers to soul and body? How often have I recourse to him in temptation or perplexity? Have I ever, in return for his unselfish devotion to me, congratulated him on his dignity and holiness and happiness? O my Good Angel, how little notice have I taken of thee in the past!

And hear his voice—The importance of this charge I cannot overrate. I can do no good of myself, yet God will not bring me to Heaven without myself. The work of my salvation is to be done betwixt Himself and me. His part is to move me by His inspirations to do what He requires of me; my part is to give heed to His Will, and with His help to carry it into effect. My Guardian Angel has to communicate His Will to me and help me to its accomplishment. Many times every day—unless my spiritual senses are dulled for want of use—I shall find him urging me to what is good, checking me when I am solicited to evil, reproving me when I have gone astray. It is by heeding the inspirations of God, prompting and warning them, that the elect will save their souls; contempt of these inspirations will be the ruin of those who perish. How docile I must be to my good Angel, how ready to hear his voice and to obey him!

And do not think him one to be contemned:—The regard that God shows for His creatures, more especially His intelligent creatures, is a sweet and wonderful mystery: "Thou being Master of power...with great favour disposest of us."[1] Quite marvellous is the reverence with which He speaks of His Angels. Their glory is to be superadded to His own on the Last tremendous Day "when the Son of Man shall come in His majesty and all the Angels with Him."[2] St. Luke says "when He shall come in His majesty and that of His Father, and of the holy Angels."[3] "Whoever shall confess Me before men, him shall the Son of Man confess before the Angels of God."[4] "I charge thee before God and Christ Jesus and the elect Angels,"[5] are the solemn words of St. Paul.

No, indeed, I may not think my Angel one to be contemned. What is it to contemn? It is to slight, to pass by with disdain or disrespect. Does my Angel feel himself dishonoured in any of these particulars?

For he will not forgive when thou hast sinned.—What! God forgives us so often and so readily, and do His Angels withhold forgiveness or follow tardily where He leads? Surely not, when they fill all Heaven with their rejoicing upon one sinner doing penance. But He would bring home to us with startling force that characteristic of the Holy Angels so prominent throughout Scripture—their absolute devotion to God and the loyalty with which they make His

---

1 Wisd. 12:18.   2 Matthew 25:31.   3 Luke 9:26.
4 Luke 12:8.   5 1 Tim. 5:21.

cause their own. "Say not before the Angel: There is no Providence."[1] "And forthwith an Angel of the Lord struck him (Herod) because he had not given the honour to God."[2]

But if thou wilt hear his voice, and do all that I speak, I will be an enemy to thy enemies, and will afflict them that afflict thee.—Hear *his* voice and do all that *I* speak. God speaks to me in my Angel's voice—a motive for prompt obedience and trust. How safe and happy I shall be if, like the Holy Angels, I am loyal always to my Creator and Lord and make His interests my own. My enemies He will make His enemies, and them that afflict me He will afflict.

See that you despise not one of these little ones—When anyone high in authority says to us: "See that you do not" this or that, we understand that a grave command is imposed upon us. Our Lord's charge to us here is very solemn. He has nothing more at heart than the welfare of these little ones who believe in Him, and He will not suffer injury to them to go unpunished. To be an occasion of harm to a child by bad example, neglect, carelessness as to its companions, amusements, books, and the like, is to incur the anger of its zealous Guardian who will not fail to denounce before God one who has hurt his little charge. Must we not be careful to have as friends, not as enemies, those who always behold the Face of God in Heaven and according to our deeds will be our accusers or our intercessors with Him!

---

1   Eccles. 5:5.   2   Acts 12:23.

VIII

"I SEND MY ANGEL"

II

WITH all reverence I may use these words and the ministry of my Good Angel to give to God a worship and service far beyond the scope of my own powers.

If I have important business on hand which I cannot despatch myself, I employ an agent, get some one with influence to interest himself in it, try to secure the help of a *persona grata* at headquarters—why should I not show a like diligence in affairs that are beyond the domain of sense?

As God's creature I must be concerned in all that affects His glory. "Thy Kingdom come," is on my lips continually, and as, oppressed by the stifling atmosphere of this world, I look up to Heaven, my wish must often be that I could give to God here and now the praise and service He will have from me one day. My place there may be empty for very many years yet—must I wait till I reach it before I can serve Him as I desire? Why? when I have one at hand only too glad to be my messenger thither and to act in my name. His spotless presence and perfect praise are always welcome there; he will adore and give thanks for me—*I will send my Angel*.

As a member of the human family I must be keenly interested in whatever concerns its welfare. Wherever my brethren are to be found, in Heaven, in Purgatory, or still in probation here, I have duties towards them, and who can help me to discharge these duties like my Guardian Angel?

To our Lady and to my Patrons and friends of whom I have so many in Heaven, he will take my congratulations and petitions.

To the Holy Waiting Souls he will bear the alms I give him for distribution among them—Masses, Communions, Indulgences, good works of various kinds, all of which will bring them relief and shorten their time of suffering.

To the forsaken Souls, forgotten by their nearest and dearest, the multitudes of whom no one thinks on earth—*I will send my Angel:*

To those near and dear to me, to whom I am bound still by the tenderest ties and duties, who look to me for help in their dire need and distress—*I will send my Angel:*

To the eager Soul nearest Heaven, to the Soul that has longest to wait, to the Soul that suffers most, to those who may be there on my account—to all these, with the help I can so easily procure them—*I will send my Angel:*

To aid the cause of Christ on earth, to enlighten those who control the destinies of the Church and of my country—*I will send my Angel:*

To strengthen the hands of priests, to remove obstacles and dangers from their path, to preserve them as the salt of the earth from taint or corruption—*I will send my Angel:*

To neutralise evil influence everywhere, especially before the unsuspecting eyes of the young, to open the eyes of those who are working with the spirits of evil for the ruin of the little ones—*I will send my Angel:*

To the slums of great and so-called Christian cities, to the densely populated regions of pagan lands, to the ignorant who need instruction, to the proudly wise and self-sufficient who need merciful humiliation, to the poor, the unsuccessful, the downtrodden, the despairing, the little children—*I will send my Angel:*

To the haunts of business and of amusement where harm in many forms may lurk, to the lonely sick in hospitals, to schoolrooms and to prisons, to the busy streets, to the fishing boats out at sea—everywhere bearing the saving inspirations of God, *I will send my Angel.*

There will be thousands of unsanctified deathbeds in the world tonight, many within call of a priest, many where no foot of priest has ever trod; the Angels there are striving with the spirits of darkness for the departing souls, too often, alas! with little or no cooperation from them or from surrounding friends. To help these zealous Guardians at this last decisive hour, to bring them such succour as will ensure the victory to grace and enable them to present their charges with joy before the Judgement seat of Christ—*I send my Angel.*

Wherever there will be sudden death today by land or sea, I will send my Angel, that at his prayer grace may be swifter still and hinder death however sudden from being unprepared.

When I find myself with others in a room, a shop, a railway carriage, a place of entertainment, I will accustom myself to call to mind the Angels there. The remembrance will be at once a protection, a check, a resource, an inspiration, a refreshment, a means of union with God. I am not likely to indulge in ill-natured gossip or criticism or to let the trivialities of life wholly monopolise the conversation when I remember who are listening—and recording. As I pass people in the streets, I will salute their Angels, so little thought of, so often saddened by our forgetfulness of God and our offences against Him.

In my relations with the poor and the suffering, and above all with little children, I will recollect the vigilance of their Angels and take heed lest word or deed of mine should be to any an occasion of harm.

When I have a decision of any importance to make, advice to give as to a step which cannot be retraced, a difficult interview to face, I will commend it to my Angel and to the Angels of those with whom I have to deal. When I find no means of reaching a soul which I earnestly desire to help, I will make friends with its Angel.

Wherever evil example, evil words, or evil writing are working ruin to souls; wherever false principles are being propagated, and pride of intellect, worldliness, love of pleasure, selfishness in any of its many forms, are choking up the avenues of grace; wherever tender ties are hindering the sacrifice for which grace calls, or souls are being lured by the prospect of temporal advantage to exchange the next world for this, eternal happiness hereafter for a good time now; wherever, in short, there is need of body or soul on the wide earth to-day—there, to plead, to enlighten and strengthen, to win the great mercies of God and His efficacious grace, I pray the Holy Angels of God to be. And there, to help forward the interests of God and of souls—*I send my Angel.*

IX

THE BOOK OF LIFE

"Whose names are in the book of life." (Philip. 4:3.)

WHAT excitement there is on the part of candidates and parents and teachers and friends on the morning when the examination results come out! What rushing to the papers, what eager scanning of the lists for the expected names! If these have earned Distinctions, if they appear in the Honours Lists, what jubilation there is all round! Congratulations fly over the world, and within their own little circle the names of those who have thus distinguished themselves are in every mouth. Where a pass only has been obtained, satisfaction takes a somewhat milder form, but, after all, the goal has been reached, efforts and toil have been rewarded, there is abundant cause for rejoicing still.

But what about the names that do not appear, the names that loving eyes seek again and again, hoping against hope—what about the failures? Perhaps the less said about these the better. Kind words and condolences only hurt, excuses fall flat, the only consolation—and that a doubtful one—is the hope of better success next time.

The contrast—seen maybe in the same home—sets one thinking of another examination, of other successes, and alas! of other failures. Of that final examination to which we must all come, St. John says: "And I saw the dead, great and small, standing in the presence of the throne, and the books were opened: and another book was opened, which is the book of life, and the dead were judged by those things which were written in the books, according to their works."[1]

Two books only, and the names of all, great and small, entered in one or other! Where will mine be?

Who dreams of presenting himself for examination without careful preparation, or supposes that one can dawdle through the year and come off with Honours by making a dash for them at the end? If we listen to the comments of teachers on successful and unsuccessful candidates, we shall find that their prophecies of success or failure are based on steady work in one case and on idleness or inertness in the other. Talent of course goes for much, but not for everything, as many are apt to suppose; there must be strenuous, persevering labour if success is to be achieved.

Are the conditions different in the work of our salvation? No. Heaven does not come to us as a matter of course, it has to be won by resolution and effort. But the effort is not beyond our strength. Nay, in many respects less is required to gain everlasting happiness than to secure the poor prizes of this life. For success here, a certain amount of talent is necessary. Goodwill alone avails nothing. The greater number of men could not pass a preliminary examination to save their life.

1 Apoc. 20:12.

But to succeed in the one thing necessary: goodwill, *i.e.*, genuine goodwill which accepts the conditions and takes the means—this is everything.

Again: the examinees of this world are kept in ignorance, if not of the matter of examination, at least of the actual questions, until the eventful hour arrives. But *we* know all our life through what will be matter for judgement—the Commandments of God and of the Church, and the duties of our state; every thought, word, and deed from the use of reason to our latest breath; the graces we have received and our correspondence; the stewardship confided to us and our discharge of its responsibilities. All this we know, and for all this we can make direct and distinct preparation hour by hour. Moreover, we can rectify mistakes and improve our prospects in a marvellous manner. Prayer, frequent and fervent recourse to the Sacraments, examination of conscience, direction, retreats, sermons, spiritual reading, not only keep our aim steadily before us, but make good our losses and sustain our energy to the end.

Another advantage we have over the candidates in the examination room is the direct power we have of controlling results. They would hardly dream of making up to the examiners with a view to obtaining a favourable verdict on their papers. *We* may approach our Judge as often as we will, and in the closest and most intimate intercourse of friendship, transact with Him the business on which our future depends. We may secure His favour, we may prevail on Him to overlook our deficiencies, we may dictate to Him our sentence.

Nor is there any fear of being ousted by rivals as in competitive examinations here; we may aim confidently at the highest; distinctions and honours to satisfy the noblest ambition may be ours—if we will.

Only—we have but one chance. If we succeed, all will be well with us through the countless ages of eternity. We shall never be put to another test, the results of our work will endure for ever. If we fail, there is no trying again, no profiting by mistakes. We have the opportunity now, as long as life shall last; we have conditions more favourable than those of millions around us; we have every help within the reach of prayer; we have time and grace at our disposal. But these will not be ours much longer. "Work while it is day," we are told, "the night cometh when no man can work."[1] And the night may fall suddenly. "Watch," says our Blessed Lord, "for you know not the day nor the hour."[2] "And what I say to you I say to all: Watch."[3] We cannot afford to hazard results; everything depends upon being ready when He calls.

And to what does He call when the labour of this short life is done?

To the holy City, the new Jerusalem, whose foundations are of precious stones and the streets of pure gold, as it were transparent glass, and the twelve gates are twelve pearls, where the Lord God is the Temple and the Lamb is the lamp thereof: to that Kingdom and Home prepared for us from the foundation of the world, of which St. John says: "There shall not enter into it anything defiled…but they that are written in the book of life of the Lamb."[4]

---

1   John 9:4.   2   Matthew 25:13.   3   Mark 13:37.
4   Apoc. 21:27.

X

"CROOKED WAYS"

THE crowds that flocked to the preaching of St. John the Baptist had four things to do to prepare for the coming Messiah. They were to bring down every mountain and hill, to fill up the valleys, to make the crooked ways straight and the rough ways plain. The same preparation is expected of us, and for us, as for the Jews, the main hindrances are the crooked ways.

"Make straight the paths of our God,"[1] Isaias said long ago. Our Lord cannot get on with a soul given to crookedness. He is not at home with it nor it with Him. Perhaps some of us know the uncomfortable feeling of talking to one whom we are trying to trick or think we have tricked. Anything like free and pleasant conversation is out of the question; the sooner the interview comes to an end, the better. So is it with us when we are not honest with God, when we are conscious of something being wrong between ourselves and Him which we have no intention of putting right, or of something He is asking of us that we will not give Him—a bad habit

---

1   Isaias 40:3.

to be broken, a dangerous pleasure to be sacrificed, a growing intimacy to be checked. Anything else He may demand, but our Agag must be spared. And He persists, and gradually a wall comes between us and Him and joy goes out of His service, for "who hath resisted Him and had peace?"[1] Our confessions become troubled; at Mass and Communion we are ill at ease, glad after a few uncomfortable prayers to hurry out of Church as if the atmosphere there oppressed us.

The reason why some of us find our intercourse with God habitually difficult may be that we hardly aim at anything more than a lip-service, and even in this there is unreality. We get into the way of saying prayers we do not mean and never shall mean. Do we really wish we could shed tears of blood over our sins, or that our heart could be torn from our body and purified in fiercest fire from all its dross? If we do, well and good; if we do not, why say so? Are we prepared to have our Purgatory in this world? If not, why pray for it?

What is the use of our protesting that we would die a thousand deaths for our Lord, when we will not go across the street for daily Mass, and again this morning broke our resolution to rise at the appointed time? Surely, in time of prayer at least we should be real; any affectation then is so ridiculously out of place that it must shut the gates of Heaven against us. No matter what we are, if we come to prayer *as we are*, we shall be welcome. The Pharisee would have been justified like the publican if, instead of recounting his good deeds, he had accused himself

---

1   Job 9:4.

of the pride and ostentation which made him odious in the sight of God. All through the Scriptures we find straightforwardness with God accepted and rewarded, but crooked ways and "lying lips an abomination to the Lord."[1] "Remove from thee a froward mouth…let thy eyes look straight on…make straight the paths for thy feet…decline not to the right hand nor to the left."[2] "A heart that goeth two ways shall not have success."[3]

"Every proud man is an abomination to the Lord,"[4] precisely because of his untruthfulness, for "pride was not made for man."[5] Of himself he is and has nothing; all that he has and is, he has received. If he glories in himself as if he had not received[6], how should he not be hateful to the God of truth! "If anyone is a little one let him come to Me,"[7] says the Truth. Such alone are invited. To whatever wisdom or maturity we have attained, we must all go to Him with the candour of little children, for His "communication is with the simple."[8]

Yet we must not keep aloof because of a feeling of insincerity in our dealings with Him, but take this, like every other form of disease, to our Heavenly Physician. Some people find themselves helplessly entangled in crooked ways and despair of ever getting free. We must not despair. Every trouble of mind and conscience we may take confidently to our God, all the subtleties of the heart which "is perverse above all things and unsearchable,"[9] an enigma to all but Him who made it.

---

1 Prov. 12:22.
2 Prov. 4:24-27.
3 Ecclus. 3:28.
4 Prov. 16:5.
5 Ecclus. 10:22.
6 1 Cor. 4:7.
7 Prov. 9:4.
8 Prov. 3:32.
9 Jerem. 17:9.

In the days of our self-delusion we believed ourselves irreproachable in one respect at least—we were genuine, straightforward, upright, above crooked dealings with God or man. Alas! alas! for our good opinion of ourselves, self-knowledge came with time and discovered to our humiliation and distress the extent to which we are made up, the amount of paint with which we presume to come masquerading before the Divine Majesty. So far from being the guileless Israelites we had imagined, we have to plead guilty to a host of little insincerities not only in our intercourse with those about us but in our dealings with God himself.

When this is the result of frailty rather than of perversity, it will not raise a barrier between us and Him, and we should make a grave mistake were we to treat ourselves as some parents and teachers are wont to treat untruthful children. Insincerity, in their eyes, denotes such depravity in the poor little delinquents, that it cannot be denounced too strongly or punished too severely. Yet it is a fault to which the generality of children are prone, and the horror and indignation it provokes may easily, by creating a false conscience, do more harm than the fault itself. A lie of excuse is in itself, and apart from the injury it may do to another, a venial sin. If by exaggerated language a timid child is led to believe it mortal, terrible results may follow. Neither must we lead a child to suppose that untruthful habits have rendered it so contemptible that all confidence has been forfeited for ever; rather must we encourage it by the reminder that this is but one of the faults to which we are all subject and that it can be conquered like all the rest.

This encouragement we must extend to ourselves when—long after we have left childhood behind us—we begin to discover our own crooked ways. Instead of visiting upon ourselves the indignation we have bestowed on others, it will be more profitable to accept the revelation without disturbance, and to feel, perhaps, a certain sympathy for the little trembling children in whom a habit of untruthfulness is so often fostered by cross-examination and severity. Once we take ourselves honestly in hand, the tricky methods to which we resort in order to gain our ends, are apt to be flashed upon us by grace to an extent which at first is not humbling only but disconcerting. Nature will without difficulty own to pride, anger, sloth even, but hardly to insincerity, and shrinks from being brought face to face with what is the direct reversal of its ideal self. It takes time and the quiet humility that grows as the process of self-knowledge advances, to be able to see without perturbation the ugliness with which we are confronted, to abase ourselves for it before God—and then, like Queen Candace's eunuch, go on our way rejoicing.

Trust in our Heavenly Father deepens with the truthfulness that, undismayed by continual lapses, takes to Him again and again one of the most humiliating of the infirmities by which our poor nature is beset. And how truthfulness and trust gain His Heart we learn from the story of the woman who pressed through the crowd to touch the hem of our Lord's garment, saying to herself: "If I shall touch only His garment I shall be healed." She came behind Him. She was afraid to be seen. He might be displeased at her boldness. But, finding He knew that virtue had gone out from Him and that she could not be hid, she came trembling and fell down at His feet, "and told Him all the truth."

This is what He loves—that we should fearlessly come to Him and tell Him *all the truth* about ourselves. It may be that there is nothing good to tell, that the truth is something we are very much ashamed of. No matter, we may trust it all to Him who is so kind, so tender, so ready to excuse when He can, and to forgive always. He will never upbraid us either in this world or the next with what we have told Him in confidence and trusted to Him by our own free act. What it is to have a friend to whom we can tell "all the truth," and what a joy that that Friend is our Judge!

More than half our difficulties in prayer come from our not being quite honest with our Lord, not telling Him all the truth about ourselves. If we were to mend in this respect, and cultivate the habit of owning to Him quite simply any fault our conscience has against us, we should find the barrier that parts Him from us breaking down. The constraint and awkwardness would go and we should be at our ease with Him. For so He has promised: "You shall know the truth and the truth shall make you free."[1]

---

1   John 8:32.

XI

MEDIOCRITY *versus* EXCELLENCE

"Be zealous for the better gifts. And I show unto you yet a more excellent way." (1 Cor. 12.)

UST we take it for granted that the practice of our faith on the low level line is the road to Heaven *for us?* Does the aim to get "just inside the door" commend itself to us as safe, as complying with St. Paul's injunction: "so run that you may obtain,"[1] as showing a grasp of the meaning of our Lord's words: "the Kingdom of Heaven suffereth violence and the violent bear it away"?[2]

St. Augustine before his conversion had earnest longings for better things, but bad habits and the fear of a hard struggle with himself held him back. One day he came upon a book which told of the conflicts and victories of the Saints. He read it. He pondered it. Conscience and grace spoke loud: his hour was come. The example of so many, weak like himself—men, women, youths, maidens, mere children, impressed him profoundly and he cried out: "These have overcome themselves and secured the Kingdom

---

1   1 Cor. 9:24.   2   Matthew 11:12.

of Heaven—and why not I?" He made his resolution; he broke finally with the past; he kept continually before him the powerful stimulus of example; he saw the Saints as they passed beneath the heavenly portals turn round and beckon to him and—he became a Saint!

That procession of holy ones never ceases; it is as full and varied and wonderful in our own days as in St. Augustine's. Young and old of every rank of life are there, differing in character, circumstances, and education, in their gifts and their graces and their trials; some innocent, others penitents; some coming to the service of God at the third hour, some at the eleventh, but all alike in the strong will to give to God their best, to consider, not what they are bound to do for Him, but what they may do. They look at themselves, soul and body, and they choose to labour first for the interests of the soul, and to compel the body, whether it will or not, so to behave that it shall help—not harm—the soul. They look at Time, they look at Eternity, and they choose to forego often and resolutely "the good things that are present"[1] lest they should forfeit those that are to come. They look at the Crucifix, at the widespread arms, the parched lips, the thorn-crowned head, the pierced hands and feet; they look into the Soul and see Its desolation and Its agony; and they resolve that their life shall be—not, indeed, an adequate return for love such as this, but the best return they can make. They will live for Him, not for themselves; they were redeemed at the same price as the Saints, they will prove their gratitude and love like the Saints.

---

1   Wisd. 2:6.

The Crucifix stands beside the path of each one of us as we go through life. It speaks, not of an act done long ago for mankind as a whole, but of Christ's personal love and sacrifice of Himself for each single soul, and of the return for such love and sacrifice for which each single soul is responsible. "All you who pass by the way attend and see."[1] It is an appeal to us one by one. It is an appeal to *me* during my short time of life here, to make such return as I may to Him who has loved me like this.

Some see that pleading Form and simply pass by. Others look and are touched for the moment, and go their way, and in the business or pleasure or excitement or cares of this life forget Christ Crucified.

And there are those who pause, and look long and earnestly; come back and look again and yet again, till at last the lesson begins to be learnt, the personal love of Christ for them individually and their personal debt to Him comes home to them; they understand now the justice and the urgency of the great Commandment: "Thou shalt love the Lord thy God with thy whole heart, and with thy whole soul, and with all thy mind, and with all thy strength," and their life's work and joy henceforth is to comply with it.

What is *my* answer to that appeal? It is *for me* He hangs there; *my sins* that agony is expiating; *my graces* here, *my glory* by and bye are being won at this tremendous price. "He loved me and delivered Himself for me."[2] And why? What am I to Him that He should love me so? What have I done to deserve such love? What am I doing, what must I do henceforth to make Him the return I ought?

1 Lament. 1:12. 2 Galat. 2:20.

So has all eminent service of God begun. God touches the soul with His grace; the soul responds. God urges us to follow, not languidly but strenuously, the traces of those whose feet were in His footprints, who made His Life their study and example, whose main desire and aim in life was to return Him love for love. They look back upon us and try to stir us to emulation: "I beseech you," they cry to us one and all, "be followers of me as I am of Christ."[1] "And make haste, make haste for the time is short."

There are times at least when we hear their voice; when we look wistfully at the Saints and wonder why we who have the same obligation and inducements to serve God faithfully and to love Him fervently, should be content with so poor a service and so halfhearted a love.

"But what is the use," some of us may say, "of taking note of aspirations which come to nothing? Who would have patience with, or put faith in, desires so inconstant as ours? We hesitate to say today what we know our acts will belie tomorrow. We wonder how the Saints contrived to keep themselves always at white heat."

Nowhere are we told that they did. They certainly had their bad days, aye, and weeks and months and years, like us. But they battled with discouragement and pushed on in spite of weariness and disgust. By trusting in Him who makes all things work together for the good of those who love Him, they came to be independent of moods and tenses. They took from His hand all seasons as they came— the brightness of one day with its hopes and desires, the dullness of weeks that followed; then a spell of sunshine

---

1   1 Cor. 4:16.

perhaps, then more mist and frost. It was the intercourse with God—easy at times, distressingly hard at others, but persevered in always and never allowed to depend on the humour of the hour—that kept them up, strengthened their good desires, won grace for the time of need, and made recourse to God and union with God natural to them at last as the air they breathed.

If, like them, we learn to confide to Him all the secrets of our wistful but inconstant hearts, we shall find that little by little will come the courage to take ourselves honestly in hand, to search out and root out our bad habits, to do violence to the Kingdom of Heaven and like the Saints bear it away. Prayer is the great lever of the spiritual life, and the Sacraments are a storehouse of grace that is simply inexhaustible. Nothing can resist them: neither bad habits, nor the force of temptation, nor long indifference, nor even grievous falls. By their means good desires grow strong enough to bear fruit, good habits are formed and matured, and the love of God begins to take full possession of the soul. Then gifts and service and sacrifice—the ways in which true love shows itself—will not be wanting. Prayer now will be, not a simple duty with its strait and well-defined limits, but the very breath of life, bringing about that habitual union with God which makes His life and action flow into our acts and, in a sense, deify them. What is to hinder us from making this experience our own?

We come across lives in which exceptional advantages—talents, education, means, influence—have been recklessly thrown away or misused. And on the other hand, we see energy and perseverance triumphing over adverse circumstances, making the most of every chance and achieving the most brilliant success. The same, but with a more momentous issue, shall we see in innumerable instances when we all stand "revealed before the Judgement seat of Christ."[1] Here, noble work has been done with meagre gifts and opportunities. There, reckless waste of grace has brought ruin irreparable on those who ought to be high up in the Kingdom of God.

Why not forestall the experiences of that Day and learn its lessons while we may profit by them! As Catholics we have received much, and much will be expected of us. We own as brothers and sisters that glorious multitude who have understood the meaning of life and have used it for the purpose for which it was given. Have we no ambition to show ourselves worthy of them? They were like us; they had their difficulties and weaknesses; more, very many of them, than our share of trial. And they have come victors out of it all! They have smoothed the way for our feet; they have left us their example, their struggles, their mistakes even, for our help and encouragement. St. Teresa dallied with grace for twenty years before she sprang forward and attained the perfection to which she was called.

"Then I may wait," someone says, "and in twenty years a great grace may come to me."

That we may not say. We cannot presume on the patience of God. He is in no way beholden to us that He should wait at our door till it suits us to open. For a while He stands and knocks; then, if we do not open to Him He passes on and seeks hospitality elsewhere. "Be not

---

1   2 Cor. 5:10.

deceived, God is not mocked."[1] He offers us His grace *now* and time wherein to use it, as He offered it to the young man who went away sorrowful, and to the thieves on Calvary. One of these seized his opportunity and is a Saint in Heaven. Of the other we only know that he missed the same opportunity, and so died.

Why should we be content with mediocrity when sanctity is within our reach? Under my hand I have the materials of sanctity. Every life provides them. Numbers in circumstances like my own are using these materials splendidly—why, oh why not I!

It is not high states of prayer, visions, ecstasies, miraculous gifts that are wanted, but such prayer as with God's help I can make, such virtues as I have daily occasions of practising, such fidelity to grace, and reception of the Sacraments, and sanctification of daily duties and daily trials as my life affords.

Some states, it is true, offer greater facilities for sanctification than others, and for that reason they are chosen. But it would be a grievous mistake to suppose that any lawful state is devoid of them. If the choice is open to me, I should choose that which, after prayer, I shall judge from my own knowledge of myself to be the best for *me*. If my state is already fixed, I have but to use the abundant means of sanctification its duties place within my reach. I need not go into a religious house to become a Saint. I need not cut myself off from intercourse with others, but in that very intercourse find my opportunities. It is not occasions that are wanting anywhere but the will to profit by them. The

1   Galat. 6:7.

wise amongst us do profit. How many busy mothers at everyone's beck and call from morning till night, how many sick in the hospitals, how many of the young with life before them, and of the aged who have outlived their work and interests here, are using their opportunities grandly and turning all into merit. In stately homes, in the slums, in multitudes of earth's obscure places, God is getting superb service from His Saints of today. A few years hence, and one here and there will be raised by the Church to her altars for the homage and encouragement of their brethren. Then those who lived by their side will come forward and bear witness to the saintly lives they saw but did not imitate.

And why did they not imitate? "Because of the labour that must be gone through in the conflict," à Kempis tells us. Yet that labour, "momentary and light"[1] purchases an eternity of rest and joy in the presence of God. And even now it has its reward in the knowledge that one soul aiming at a perfect service gives more glory to God than a multitude who are content with mediocrity, and wins a nearness to Him, the happiness of which far outweighs any pains by which it has been earned.

Shall we not surrender ourselves to grace? There is yet time. Prayer and patience and persevering effort to follow the lead of the Holy Spirit will ensure that service and win that reward.

> Be docile to thine unseen Guide,
> Love Him as He loves thee,
> Time and obedience are enough,
> And thou a Saint shalt be.[2]

1　2 Cor. 4:17.　　　2　Faber

A Priest's Dream[1]

The doctor said I could not live till morning. I lay in a lethargy, to all appearance dead. Now and again my attendant came in to see if I was still living.

Suddenly, all sense of pain left me. I found myself encompassed with the thickest darkness, a darkness that was appalling. After a while, light began to break in upon me, seemed to approach me, grew and grew till it became a dazzling brightness. In the midst I discerned the form of a young man of extraordinary beauty, clothed in white. Without speaking, he made me a sign to follow him, and instantly I was transported away from earth into limitless space. Stars above, below, on every side; no sun nor moon but stars everywhere. I seemed to be travelling along a high embankment such as the railway line runs along at times, but all of cloud. My Angel Guardian, for such I understood him to be, led me on in silence. He seemed absorbed in thought and disinclined to speak. On and on we went till at length I ventured to say: "Where am I going?" He answered shortly, and as I thought, not very pleasantly: "To Heaven."

Presently we came to a vast staircase, immense in width, higher than the highest of mountains and lost at the upper end among the clouds. We began to ascend the steep steps, my Angel passing on before me. After two hours or

---

1 The Catechism warns us against giving heed to "omens, dreams, and such like fooleries." But there is nothing to prevent us heeding and profiting by anything which strikes us as more than the nightly vagaries of our unguided brain. Cardinal Newman at the age of nineteen had a dream which was a help to him to the end of his life. And not a few of us have had a like experience.

so spent thus I summoned up courage to say: "How worn these steps are!" He answered in the same laconic manner: "They may well be worn, for millions have passed this way."

Again we ascended in silence. At length he paused suddenly and turning to me said: "O child, you should have seen the procession that passed this way last night, to meet and welcome according to his merits a man of no account on earth, unlettered, uncouth, but held in reverence in Heaven as one who has laboured and suffered much for the Lord our God. When he came to the staircase you are mounting you should have seen how Archangels and the highest Princes of Heaven went down to meet him. He had never come in for honours on earth and did not know how to receive them. They bore him along in their midst in triumph. As he passed on, tens of thousands came forth from Heaven to show him reverence. They cleared a way for him, they bowed down before him, they kissed the hem of his garment, whilst he, amazed beyond belief, sought to evade the marks of their reverent affection. O my child, you should have seen that entry into Heaven of one who had suffered much for God. You should have seen and heard when the Son of Man, before His Father and before the Angels of God confessed him for one of His. You should see now the nearness to the Throne of God that for eternity will be his."

I looked up. The Angel's face was aglow with a heavenly enthusiasm; the tones of his voice thrilled me through and through. A new light broke in upon me. I fell on my knees before him: "Take me back to earth," I cried, "get me a little longer span of life, that I may sacrifice myself for the love and service of God and win nearness to Him in the life to come!"

With this I awoke. I was better. In a few weeks I was about again, but—*a changed man:* that dream or vision had altered my life.

XII

HAIL MARY

HAIL! a word of reverent salutation. Admiration, enthusiasm, love, are all contained in it, but reverence predominates. It cannot be said thoughtfully without the reverence of the heart passing to the lips. Is this beautiful salutation on my lips what it ought to be?

Reverence is at a discount in these days. We see less and less of it in each succeeding generation, less in children, servants, dependents generally; less in equals, less in friends; less, painfully less, in intercourse with parents and with priests—less, worst of all, in our dealings with God.

The free and easy ways with those above us, now in vogue, have nothing mischievous about them, some will say; they are merely the outcome of the liberty which the spirit of the age grants to all; they imply no want of refinement in the mind or of affection in the heart, and endanger neither respect nor love.

Supposing anything could be urged in defence of the growing want of reverence that marks intercourse among ourselves, nothing can excuse its absence in our relations with God. Here it is simply indispensable. It is the attitude of every rational creature in His Presence, more and more profound in the heavenly hierarchies as they approach Him more nearly; in the Archangels than in the Angels; deeper yet in the Seraphim; the highest Angel cannot reach its depths in the soul of Mary; the sacred human Soul of Jesus is steeped in it, "who in the days of His flesh…was heard for His reverence."[1]

How, then, can any other attitude befit us or be tolerated in us! Those who should transgress the etiquette of Courts would be hustled from the royal presence! Reverence is the essential condition of approach to the King of kings. Do we bring it with us always when we come to prayer? Are we a fit and acceptable companion to our holy and reverent Angel Guardian when we kneel down to pray?

The Angels teach us many lessons—none, perhaps more impressively than this of reverence. "Thousands of thousands minister to Him, and ten thousand times a hundred thousand stand before Him."[2] "And all the angels stood round about the throne…and they fell down before the throne upon their faces and adored God."[3]

Next to the throne of God is the throne of the Mother of God. After the reverence due to Him, is the veneration due to her whose titles and prerogatives almost exceed belief—Mother of God, Mother of our Creator, Virgin Mother, Mother of Divine Grace, Queen of Angels, Queen of All Saints, Queen of Heaven! "Choose," says St. Bernard, speaking of the Divine Maternity, "which you will most admire, the incomprehensible condescension of the Son or

1   Heb. 5:7.   2   Dan. 7:10   3   Apoc. 7:11.

*"And they came with haste; and they found Mary and Joseph,
and the infant lying in the manger."* (Luke 2:16.)

the incomparable dignity of the Mother." To her was given more grace than to all Angels and men beside. After her divine Son she is the masterpiece of God's hand, as Mother of all the living, the Dispenser of His grace to the whole Church and to each individual soul. Should we speak with the tongues of men and of Angels, we could not duly proclaim her dignity nor sound her praise.

Must we not at least approach her with reverence? The tender and familiar love and confident recourse to her in every need, which as her children we are allowed, must never make us forget the reverence with which even an Archangel was bidden by God Himself to salute her, "Hail, full of grace!" said Gabriel, before whose majesty the prophet Daniel had fallen on his face trembling, and the just Zachary was filled with fear.

There is reverence in his every word and act; in the way in which he removes her trouble at such exalted praise, and replies to her question, and satisfies her doubt, and magnifies the "Holy" who is to be born of her; and—his mission fulfilled, her "Fiat" secured, the great Mystery accomplished, his act of adoration paid—leaves her instantly, silently, without one word of homage or congratulation, alone with her God and her Son.

Might it not help us in the first Joyful Mystery of the Rosary, to place ourselves humbly in a corner of the little room at Nazareth at the hour of the Annunciation, and watch the Angel's entrance, and note his attitude, his tone, his glowing reverent face, and learn from him how to say, what it was his privilege to teach all generations to say: *Hail Mary!*

…"Now raise thy view
Unto the visage most resembling Christ:
For in her splendour only shalt thou win
The power to look on Him." Forthwith I saw
Such floods of gladness on her visage shower'd
From holy spirits, winging that profound,
That whatsoever I had yet beheld
Had not so much suspended me with wonder
Or shown me such similitude of God.
And he, who had to her descended once
On earth, now hail'd in heaven, and on poised wing,
"Ave Maria, Gratia Plena," sang:
To whose sweet anthem all the blissful court
From all parts answering, rang, that holier joy
Brooded the deep serene.[1]

---

1   *Paradise*. Canto XXXII. Dante.

XIII

"US ALSO"

"Master, in saying these things Thou reproachest us also."
(Luke 11:45.)

E can hear the indignant tone of these lawyers. The Master's implied rebuke was unintentional no doubt. That He should presume to include them in His reproaches was not to be thought of, but He must be more circumspect; His words were open to misconstruction and might lessen the reverence due to them as the people's teachers and guides.

So little they knew themselves. Or rather, so alarmed were they lest others should know them! All their concern was to stand well with the crowd, to be the objects of special veneration for a sanctity of which they knew themselves to be utterly destitute. What they were before God mattered little, but a slight that lowered them in the eyes of men was resented as an intolerable injury.

Is there anything of this spirit in us? Are we never piqued at a word in a sermon that points our way, an insinuation that hurts our self-respect, especially if conscience has thrust it home? It is fitting, of course, that people should be instructed from the pulpit and reminded of their failings, but propriety requires the repression of whatever might make our conduct the subject of adverse criticism, of any blame that might be supposed to include *us also*.

How did our Lord meet this display of the pride and hypocrisy He detests? How did He, who had nothing but words of tender reassurance for the public sinner, deal with these self-righteous men? Because they resented His censure of the Pharisees as a rebuke to themselves, He singled them out for special denunciation as severe as it was just. Before the eyes of the simple people whom they had deceived, He unveiled their hypocrisy, their cruelty, their hardness of heart: "Woe to you lawyers also!" Again and again came those words, terrible in themselves and made unspeakably awful by the wrath in His eye, in His bearing, in the tones of His voice.

How odious in His sight is the self-sufficiency that never owns itself in fault! Better by far sit down humbly among our fellow sinners, and accept, from whatever source it comes, the blame that is our due, than by whitewashing ourselves become a mark for special condemnation. For "God resists the proud and gives His grace to the humble."[1]

---

1   James 4:6.

XIV

"WHO IS MY NEIGHBOUR?"

(Luke 10:29.)

THE lawyer who asked our Lord, tempting Him, what he must do to possess eternal life, was asked in his turn: "What is written in the law, how readest thou?" He made answer: "Thou shalt love the Lord thy God with thy whole heart, and with thy whole soul, and with all thy strength, and with all thy mind, and thy neighbour as thyself." Jesus said to him: "Thou hast answered right, this do and thou shalt live." But he, willing to justify himself, said to Jesus: "And who is my neighbour?"

In the parable which was the reply to this question, we cannot but notice that those called "neighbours" by our Lord are not by any means such as we ordinarily understand by the term—not persons living near one another, not brought together by work in common in any of the relations of social life, but utter strangers, separated by fierce and long-standing differences, racial and religious, who might have been supposed to have no mutual duties.

It is these whom our Lord declares to be neighbours, and should any such be in need, they are to be assisted even at great inconvenience and expenditure of time, money, personal service and sacrifice.

In the tender-hearted Samaritan, our Lord gives us a model of the charity that prefers work to talk; that instead of offering useless advice to those in trouble, bestirs itself and is really helpful; that sacrifices its own convenience to the needs of others; that *shows* kindness, whatever feelings may be—and then He says to each one of us: "Go and do thou in like manner."

Do we think enough of these "neighbours" of ours, with whom circumstances so often bring us into contact, and who are waiting for us to pass by in order to receive the help they need? In a railway carriage, in church, among our visitors or servants, in a hundred unsuspected places, we may find our needy neighbour.

"But surely," it may be urged, "we are not called upon to obtrude ourselves upon the notice of strangers with unseasonable advice or help! such interference would be deservedly resented."

No, certainly, we are not invited to be either tiresome or officious, but only to have the quick eye with which charity and zeal note needs and opportunities that many never see—a stranger, evidently a Protestant, coming night after night to church during a mission without a book or clue to the service, religious questions started in the train by inquirers apparently sincere, a street accident where the sufferer is an Irishman and presumably a Catholic—are but samples of the cases in which we may step in and help.

What hinders many of us, is either an altogether inadequate idea of our obligations to our neighbour, as our Lord understands them; or, on the other hand, an exaggerated notion of the qualifications needed for efficient help; or ill-timed shyness; or the fear of meeting with a rebuff; or simply the want of interest in the souls with which we are brought into contact day by day. Now none of these difficulties occurred to the Samaritan whom our Lord sets before us as a model. He was not sent but "went up" to the wounded man by the roadside. If we wait for formal introductions, or distinct invitations on the part of those we might assist, we shall do nothing. And suppose we do meet with a repulse now and again— what then? If out of a hundred cases we succeeded once, it would be well worth while, for think what it is to be able to help one soul! Of course we must not be indiscreet, but oh! if we knew the possibilities that lie in the way of those quick to see and profit by them—on a visit, during a holiday ramble, at a *table d'hôte*, we should be on the alert always, ready for any opportunity God may send us for furthering His designs.

Prayer, at least, is always safe. If we are afraid to venture farther, we need have no hesitation here. There is often an instinctive feeling that a soul needs help, there may be no opening for a word, but prayer is always at hand, and is always safe.

But there are occasions without number when precautions of this kind are not called for, when the need is manifest and volunteers are welcome. Can we not do something for those whose faith is exposed to many temptations? See how ready others are for self-sacrifice in order to help souls; how they give time, talent, tact, to make pleasant evenings for those who might else be driven to seek dangerous amusement elsewhere. Some kind of pleasure we must all have, but those who get a great deal are apt to forget that all around them are hundreds who scarcely know what rest and holiday mean. Yet they need both, and if we do not exert ourselves, they may look for relaxation where it may hurt them to find it. Must not we who have the leisure, provide it for them where they may enjoy it with safety? Must we not call in our ingenuity to help the overworked priests in contriving an outing for the Children of Mary, a treat for the choir, a feast for the school children and the like?

These are days when the laity must come forward with whatever they can bring to the service of the great cause, if souls are to be saved. If we listen, we shall hear them cry out to us like Peter sinking in the stormy sea: "*Doth it not concern thee that we perish?*" If we listen, we shall hear the Heart of Christ crying to us from the Cross: "*I thirst!*" Can we not do something for Him? He has toiled and suffered for souls till His last breath; can we not help Him who can do no more?

A suggestive question to put to ourselves is: "Suppose everyone were to understand the precept—precept, mind, not counsel of Christ—in this matter, and to act upon it as I do, and were to use their opportunities as I use mine, what would the results be to the Catholic cause; would the Church and needy souls have reason to rejoice, or otherwise?"

XV

HARD PRAYER

"Thou turnedst away Thy face from me and I became troubled." (Ps. 29:8.)

EATHER, we are told, seems to have no influence upon wireless telegraphy; rain, fog, snow, and wind fail to obstruct. Through all, the oscillations of the electromagnetic waves set up in the transmitter fall upon the receiver tuned in sympathy with it, coherence follows, currents are excited and the signals made.

Would it were so with the obstructions we meet in prayer from our ever-varying moods! There are times when our mind comes into contact immediately and as it were naturally with heavenly things; the soul allies herself readily with the spiritual realities to which she is akin and finds joy and refreshment in them. Such happy prayer glorifies God and is pleasing to Him: "He that adoreth God with joy shall be accepted and his prayer shall approach even to the clouds."[1]

But there are times—and how often they come! when

---

1 Ecclus. 35:20.

no effort avails to bring us into relation with the unseen world. Our soul seems to be of the earth earthly, so enslaved by the senses, so dragged down by the body of clay, that the ascendancy of its spiritual nature is indiscernible. Its faculties remain inert and refuse to be won or driven. No consideration we can bring to bear upon them takes effect; the rain, fog, snow, and wind of psychological regions effectually intercept communication between us and the objects we try in vain to reach.

This state of things is disheartening, yet it can and must be utilised, for it is of frequent recurrence in the spiritual life and if not used aright, will bring with it the temptation to abandon prayer.

We have to bear in mind that it has its advantages. It comes under the "all things" which, according to St. Paul, "work together for the good of them that love God."[1] It is an enormous help to the gaining of humility, and humility at once brings the soul into communication with God: "the prayer of him that humbleth himself shall pierce the clouds and…will not depart till the Most High behold."[2] We may note, by the way, that the very same promise of piercing the clouds is made to humble as to joyful prayer.

To humble ourselves when in this helpless state should not be hard, and no other disposition is needed to bring God near. And near to help. "The Lord will not be slack… and He shall delight the just with His mercy."[3]

Because of the virtues this painful prayer calls forth, it is wonderfully meritorious. Who does not love to be

---

1 Rom. 8:28.   2 Ecclus. 35:21.   3 Ecclus. 35:22, 25.

with God if He but shows His Face, if He lifts the veil ever so little? It is the hiding of that Face that plunges us into darkness and distress: "Thou turnedst away Thy face from me and I became troubled," says David[1], and his experience is common to us all. All who are to stand before the Face of God for ever have to bear the passing pain of this eclipse. We take up the Life of one Saint after another and invariably come upon this phase of their spiritual training. No matter how short or innocent or uneventful to outward seeming their course may be, this universal law will be found worked out in it sooner or later.

Is there not some consolation for us here? To find ourselves sharing in one particular at least—and that an indispensable one—the experience of all the Saints, is cheering, provided we behave like them under the trial, content to serve God for a while at our own cost; to love Him for what He is, rather than for what He gives; to stay unweariedly knocking at His door; to give Him what we can, poor as it may be; patient with Him and with ourselves, and resolute in our determination to cling steadfastly to prayer, no matter how long or how painful the time of trial may be.

"*Expect the Lord, do manfully, and let thy heart take courage and wait thou for the Lord.*"[2]

"*Wait on God with patience, join thyself to Him and endure.*"[3]

---

1 Ps. 29:8.   2 Ps. 26:14.   3 Ecclus. 2:3.

"Wait for His mercy and go not aside from Him lest you fall." [1]

"The Lord is only for them that wait upon Him."[2]

And we will make answer:

"My heart hath said to Thee: My face hath sought Thee; Thy face, O Lord, will I still seek."[3]

"Reward them that patiently wait for Thee...and hear the prayers of Thy servants."[4]

---

1   Ecclus. 2:7.   2   Ecclus. 34:22.   3   Ps. 26:8.
4   Ecclus. 36:18.

XVI

"WHO IS THIS?"

"Who is this that cometh up from the desert, flowing with delights, leaning upon her beloved?" (Cant. 8:5.)

SUCH was the cry of admiration with which Heaven greeted its Queen; the cry of the Holy Angels to whom the Feast of her Assumption, as the Church tells us,[1] brought special joy.

Their gaze had followed her with ever-increasing wonder through the years of her life on earth. They saw the magnificence with which, in view of her future dignity, she was dowered from the first. They saw the perfect fidelity with which she traded with her immense treasure from the earliest moment of a long life to the latest. Not an instant lost through all those years; every duty accomplished as perfectly as was possible; every grace utilised to the utmost; every opportunity profited by to the full; every cross embraced with absolute conformity and love; every virtue practised with a purity and perfection attained by no other mere creature. And glorious and marvellous above all these graces and gifts,

---

1   Introit for the Feast of the Assumption.

they saw the humility which beheld in her only the handmaid of the Lord in whom it had pleased Him to do great things.

Great things on earth, great things in Heaven. So great, that the Blessed spirits as they flocked out to meet her exclaimed in astonishment: "Who is this?"

Is this the lowly one of Nazareth, the spouse of the carpenter? Is this she who laid her hands so gladly to humble household work; who hid away when the whole world went after her Divine Son; who took no part in His triumphs, but came forth and claimed Him in His disgrace? Is this she whose life was one long martyrdom; whose soul was pierced with seven swords; who knew on Calvary the cruellest of partings the world has ever seen; whose heart was rent with anguish as never mother's heart before or since? Is it the same who now comes to us as a Queen, flowing with delights, Empress of Heaven and earth, "called from Libanus to be crowned?"[1]

"Who is this?"

We look forward a few years and see another reception into the Heavenly Kingdom—our own. We see ourselves led by our faithful Angel Guardian through the Eternal Gates and met and welcomed by the Angelic host. They love these receptions and are always ready to pour out in their myriads to meet each lowly soul that comes to swell their ranks. And now it is mine they come to receive. How surprised I am at their reverent as well as affectionate greeting, at their cry of admiration: "Who is this?"

---

1   Cant. 4:8.

Is this the soul so long halting between two ways,[1] so weak and fickle, brave in resolution and faltering in execution; so low in its aspirations, so strangely inconsistent, so dearly loved by our Lord God, and so fearful of doing too much for Him in return; so ready to mete out its service, abridge its prayer, dole out its alms; so afraid of a little labour, so terrified of the Cross? Is this she who was a prey to so many fears, who found it hard to trust in God and abandon herself wholly to His Will? Who is this? The same we have watched and yearned over and prayed to see with us one day safe on this blessed shore?

Our Angel makes reply:

"Yes, it is the same. Weak and fearful and falling often, this child of mine has held fast to prayer. Her sorrow for sin has been sincere and lifelong; she has risen promptly after a fall; she has renewed her strength by frequent recourse to the holy Sacraments, and gently, gradually, they have lifted her above the low plane of spiritual selfishness to a larger, broader, happier service of God because freed from the thralldom of mere self-seeking. She has stretched out her hand to the poor and needy; she has not waited till work for God was thrust upon her but has gone out to seek it; she has helped many a fellow traveller by the way, shared many a burden, prevented many a fall. The cleansing fires have done the rest. And now we are on our way to the embrace of the Bridegroom and to the Coronation!"

---

1   3 Kings 18:21.

XVII

LEST WE FORGET

"Oh how great and honourable is the office of priests!"
(*Imitation of Christ,* Book 4, chapter 2.)

E are surprised when a soldier or one serving on board a submarine tells us of the amount of time and pains spent daily in cleaning and polishing the various parts of their equipment. "Surely," we say, "there can be no need to have everything so spic and span!"

Yet those who ought to know best tell us it is indeed necessary. The constant action of the atmosphere, and the deterioration consequent on daily use, or the accidental injury to which these things are liable—all this calls for continual supervision if they are to be kept in working order and found reliable when called for.

So is it with the things of Faith. They have to be passed in review, examined and refurbished, or they will either become useless by neglect, or blunted by familiarity. Our spiritual duties—prayer, morning and evening; the Sacraments, Mass, daily examination of conscience; our duties to others and to ourselves, require constant attention. Like the Psalmist we must be able to say: "My soul is always in my hands."[1]

Constant contact with holy things helps or harms just in proportion to the brightness or dullness of our faith. And one point which we shall do well not to omit from occasional review, is our duty to priests and the way in which we think and speak of them.

If there were but one priest in the world, à Kempis says, what reverence would he not inspire? Yet the dignity of the priesthood is not lessened because it is shared by many.

"True," we shall be told, "but there are priests and priests."

Undoubtedly; and it is precisely because of the human element that exists in greater or less prominence everywhere, that we have to enliven our faith, and penetrate beneath the surface, or rise above mere externals, to see things from its standpoint. God's dispensations might have been different from what they are. He might have willed to offer sacrifice, and absolve and communicate us, through the ministry of Angels. It is enough for us to know that He has chosen other means, to be satisfied that these means are best. We think, perhaps, that angelic ministry would have inspired us always with the awe and reverence due to their office. Alas! should not a little self-knowledge convince us of the contrary? We get used to the most astounding mysteries. We know God is really present upon our altars and within our breasts, and we can hardly produce in ourselves the faintest response to what we believe. It is not so much our fault as our misfortune

---

1   Ps. 118:109.

that use has this tendency to deaden perception. But the apathy becomes faulty and harmful when we neglect the means by which faith is roused, and without which it lies dormant and, to a certain extent, inefficacious.

We must dwell thoughtfully on the wonderful fact of the Real Presence. We must pass beyond appearances to the sublime realities of the Mass and the Sacraments, and to the stupendous dignity of those chosen ministers to whom is committed an office denied to Angels.

And just as our merit, as we kneel before Christ hidden on the altar, is in proportion to our faith, so is it in our dealings with those who serve the altar. If our intercourse with them is to be fruitful to ourselves and to others, it must be inspired by faith. It may be doubted perhaps, whether in any other matter the exercise of faith presents more practical difficulties. The vocation which raises them to such an incomparable height does not thereby transform them. The influences of home, education, environment, character and temptation, tell upon them as upon ourselves; and trials and difficulties special to their calling, which they alone can appreciate rightly, and which an inviolable secret compels them to bear alone, have effects which they would be superhuman to escape entirely. It must be so, and is so because God has thus ordained things for our good.

The great Apostle is never tired of drawing our attention to the marvellous fruits of faith. The heights to which it attains in each soul is the measure of the soul's worth in God's sight. And faith is meritorious precisely because of the difficulties which it surmounts.

Let us think of this in our dealings with priests. Let us reflect on their dignity till we have laid in our souls a foundation of reverence that nothing can destroy. Not the evidences of human frailty, nor the sadder results of temptation to which by their very ministry they are exposed, can justify our making them the butt of thoughtless and harmful speech. "Touch not my anointed, and do no evil to My prophets,"[1] is a command we cannot too earnestly take to heart. Justice to them, justice to others—to say nothing of the consequences to ourselves—forbids us to give utterance to every idle and inconsiderate thought that crosses our mind. What right have we to criticise a sermon, or an act of his ministry of which the priest alone is the competent judge? By what privilege are we entitled to destroy his people's trust in him, to restrict their alms, to plant suspicion, to spread tales, to render individuals unfriendly or even positively hostile? By what authority do we question the prudence of his guidance of others, or encourage frivolous talk about that sacred tribunal where the priest sits as judge, and the penitent's duty is humble self-accusation at the time—*and silence afterwards?*

Who shall tell the harm done to souls and the cruel injustice to priests by the retailing of advice adapted to individual need and in no wise intended for general application? If the duty of restitution binds wherever character has been injured, what shall we say of its obligation when the victim has been a priest? Fear, in the absence of any other sufficient check, should restrain

1 1 Par. 16:22, Ps. 104:15.

our tattling tongues, which in a couple of minutes may do harm that is simply irreparable.

Though we may have little to reproach ourselves with on this head, occasional self-examination may not be out of place. The spirit of reverence in any of its manifestations is no characteristic of our times, and in a matter where, for our own sake and the sake of all about us, it becomes a distinct duty to cultivate *and to show it*, we shall do well to give it now and then a few moments' serious thought— lest we forget.

XVIII

GIVE US THIS DAY OUR DAILY BREAD

I T IS the cry of children, spontaneous, at times clamorous. They ask, not for rich, savoury food, but for that which is the staff of life—bread—and they ask it daily for the supply of each day's need.

For another Bread, too, we cry: the Bread of the strong, by which we live for ever, and it is a true instinct which bids us ask for It daily.

Father, give us this day our daily bread. The father is the bread-giver; round him the hungry children crowd and cry. Our Father who art in Heaven, who "openest Thy hand and fillest with blessing every living creature,"[1] "who givest food to the young ravens that call to Thee,"[2] "are not we of more value than they"?[3]

Give us—it is the children's right to have for the mere asking. They do not beg nor buy, for the father knows their need. Our Father in Heaven not only gives but presses upon us this divine Food, and reproaches us when we hang back from Him: "You will not come to Me

---

1 Ps. 144:16.   2 Job 38:41.   3 Matt. 6:26.

that you may have life."[1]

Give us—we say. And at once the table is spread and we are bidden to take our places there. No long preparation is needed. "Open thy mouth and eat what I give thee,"[2] "and passing, He will minister to them."[3]

This day. What does it bring us? What will it ask of us? One day will bring the summons Home. Every day brings its work and its burdens, its responsibilities, its choices and decisions. This day will ask of us fidelity and sacrifice, and these things need strength—Father, "give us this day our daily Bread!"

Our daily bread. For we are Thy children, the bread of the household is ours. We ask for our own; for Its excellence It is called the Bread of Angels, but It is prepared for us— Father, "give us always this Bread."[4]

Daily bread. It might have been given under some costlier form but then we should not have been invited daily. Our Lord would have it in the form of bread—common, simple food, easily procured, the food of which we do not tire, the food of all alike, to take from us any excuse for absenting ourselves from our Father's table. He draws us thither by promises and threats. He insists upon the Food He has prepared being meant for daily use—"give us *this day our daily* bread." Its infinite value must not frighten us. For It is prepared on purpose for us, to meet our daily need, to be the sanctification of each day; to strengthen us to take up its burdens easily; to meet bravely its difficulties and its trials; to supernaturalize its joys; that we may live by Christ

---

1   John 5:40.   2   Ezech. 2:8.   3   Luke 12:37.
4   John 6:34.

whom we have received, and by Him, with Him, in Him, pass safely through its dangers and deserve its rewards.

Father, give us this day our daily Bread. And give us, for Thou canst, something beyond even this Unspeakable Gift—the light to know better Its infinite worth, to prize It more, and to show our appreciation and gratitude, not by neglecting It, under any of the foolish and false pretexts that indifference will suggest, but by receiving It humbly and often, bringing such preparation as we are able.

XIX

"ALL THY WAYS ARE PREPARED"

(Judith 9:5.)

AND the preparation was from eternity. Through uncounted ages, when no sound broke the stillness of the eternal years, when God was not yet Creator, even then we existed in the Divine Mind, with our distinct place in Time and in God's universal plan. The beauty of His finished work was to depend for certain details on our free cooperation. We and no other were to render Him the special service He would ask at our hands.

All was special about us—circumstances, helps, trials, friendships, work, successes, disappointments, opportunities, vocation, graces; designed and chosen one and all by God Himself to be instruments for the realisation of His ideal as to our individual soul.

It was not a soul simply, or any soul that God brooded over from eternity with the love of Father, Mother, Creator, Brother, Bridegroom, all in one. It was not any work that was to be made ready to our hands, or any path on which our feet were to be set. But all was prepared, Divine

Wisdom and Divine Love combining in the Providence which foresaw and ordained all, even to the smallest detail of our life, "reaching from end to end mightily and ordering all things sweetly."[1]

Why the way is level here and sheltered, brightened with flowers and made delightful by the companionship of those we love, why further on it crosses a desert waste, dips into a dark valley, skirts a precipice, or climbs a weary height, we may not know now, but this we know—that wherever it goes it is prepared, with what solicitude, with what tender provision for our need we shall see one day when we look down upon it from our place in Heaven.

We shall not wish that it had been ordered otherwise, that the hills had been lowered or the valleys filled for us, the crooked ways made straight or the rough ways plain. "He hath done all things well!" we shall cry in thanksgiving and joy. "Oh that I had known sooner the things that were for my peace, that I had realised what my faith taught me, and without misgiving, without questioning had abandoned myself to the Love that from eternity had prepared all my way!"

---

1   Wisd. 8:1.

X X

"TOLLE LEGE!"

HAD Plato, or Aristotle, or Socrates, those seekers after truth, been told that Truth Itself had come upon earth and founded a school that was to embrace all mankind, and given His doctrine by word of mouth, and followed it up by His own example; had they learned that four among His disciples had committed to writing His Life and teaching, with the rules of conduct He had left for the guidance of His followers, how eager would they have been to study that Life and doctrine, and to possess themselves of any fragments of those writings by which they might learn His spirit and form themselves upon it!

The first Christians made great account of such portions of the Scriptures, of the Gospels especially, as they could obtain. The daily study of the Holy Books was enjoined upon their disciples by the founders of the earliest monasteries. In all ages they have been light, food, remedy, refreshment, and comfort to the servants of God. It was by the study of their Divine Model in the Gospels that the Saints grew into His likeness; it is by this study we must all gain that resemblance to Him which is the mark of the predestinate: "those whom He foreknew He also predestinated to be made conformable to the image of His Son."[1] "It hath not yet appeared what we shall be," says St. John, "but we know that we shall be like Him."[2]

The likeness has to be acquired here; to bring it out more and more perfectly in ourselves, life and time are granted us; the degree in which we shall have achieved it when death comes, will be the measure of our eternal reward.

If, then, the hallmark of sanctity is likeness to Christ, if a certain measure of conformity is necessary even for salvation, ought we not to make the study of our Lord's Life and words and actions, of His virtues and spirit and character, as revealed to us in the Holy Gospels, one of our regular occupations?

"We have no time." Yet we have time for dress and amusement, for the skating-rink, for golf, and "bridge," and novel-reading, and visits, and a thousand trivialities which enter into our day.

We find time for reading the papers and the latest books out, spiritual books even, provided they are new and entertaining. We are ashamed to own to ignorance when there is question of the doings of some celebrity, of whom the world began to talk only yesterday and who will be ousted by rivals tomorrow from the place he holds today. But the Life of Him who has changed the face of the world, whose influence extends not only through all time, but through the ages of eternity, whose Life is a series of the most marvellous events recorded by history, whose character is the most beautiful, whose work the most enduring earth has ever seen—this we find insipid. We

1 Rom. 8:29.   2 1 John 3:2.

hear fragments of it read in church from time to time, and this seems to us sufficient.

But is it? Does any student use his textbook thus? Does the photographer trust to his picture coming out all right when he neglects the proper means for developing it? Is it safe to do as little as we can to ensure a place amongst those who are to be near their Lord for ever because they have made themselves like Him? And—for a higher, more unselfish motive must appeal to us—is it grateful to neglect the study of a Life lived solely for our instruction, and example? *We* see what kings and prophets and pagan sages desired to see. We can each of us say with St. Paul: "I live in the faith of the Son of God who loved me and delivered Himself for me."[1] Because we love Him and desire to love Him daily more and more, we shall prize the revelation of Himself which in the Holy Gospels He makes to us, and use it to the end for which it was given.

Knowledge and love grow together and one is the measure of the other. Were we to study for five minutes daily the record of those blessed three and thirty years, we should find a change for the better in our relations with Him before many months were past. Mass, and Communion, and Benediction, and Visits to Him in the Blessed Sacrament, would be different. Faith, Hope, and Charity would take quite a new development in our souls; we should begin to say to ourselves in joyful surprise: "*I know* in whom I have believed."[2]

---

1 Gal. 2:20.   2 2 Tim. 1:12.

XXI

BEFORE CONFESSION

"And now, O Lord Almighty, the soul in anguish and the troubled spirit crieth to Thee." (Baruch 3:1.)

IN ANGUISH, because of the multitude of my sins; because of their singular malice as *my* sins; because of the ingratitude of a child so specially beloved. In anguish, because my heart is hard and insensible when it should be broken with sorrow. Surely there is a contrition on which Thy fatherly eye rests in abundant pity—the grief that has no tears, that finds no assurance of its reality, either in a keen appreciation of the malice of sin, or of the love that has remitted the penalties sin has deserved, or of the need of reparation.

St. Augustine tells us he found more happiness in the tears he shed over his past life than in any pleasure it had brought him. How we envy him those tears—we to whom the strongest motives for sorrow appeal so feebly! O Human Heart of Christ, broken for our sins, can Thy fellow feeling for us in all things reach even to this, that the pain of insensibility should be a further claim to Thy sympathy and Thy help? Thanks be to Thee for the account

Thou dost make of our will and of our desires. These at least we can, to some extent, control. We can wish we had never sinned. We can desire to have the sorrow of David and of Peter, of Magdalen, of Augustine, and of all true penitents. And though we can give no guarantee that we shall not sin again, we can unite our will to Thine now, with the resolve promptly and trustfully to renew this union whenever any infidelity has slackened our hold on Thee. In our confessions we can renew our sorrow for past sin, now of this period of our life, now of that, and so purify our soul more and more with the waters of true contrition. In our Communions we can cling to Thee, if not with sensible devotion, with the fervour of the will which is in our power always, with the determination to shun, with Thy help, even the least deliberate sin. Thus may union with Thee become so constant and so strong, that in our measure we may be able to say with the confidence of thy blessed Apostle: "What shall separate us from the love of Christ?"[1]

---

1   Rom. 8:35.

XXII

GOD WITH US

"Who will give Thee to me for my Brother?" (Cant. 8:1.)

THE observance by the Jews of the great Commandment of the Law: "Thou shalt love the Lord thy God with thy whole heart and with thy whole soul, and with thy whole strength,"[1] a command given amidst thunder and lightning, and fire, and darkness, and the noise of the trumpet, must have been difficult. At least so it seems to us who live under the Law of Love. And how imperfectly, as far as we can gather, it was observed. Here and there we find marvellous examples of fidelity to God's commands, zeal for his worship, resignation to His Will. But a personal love that absorbed the whole soul—where shall we look for this? Was it even possible? Even in the tenderest manifestations of His Providence there was nothing for the grateful heart to leap up to and embrace in its thankfulness. Afar off, "inhabiting light inaccessible,"[2] He dwelt, where fear, indeed, and reverent worship could reach Him, but familiar love, hardly.

1   Deut. 6:5.   2   1 Tim. 6:16.

The hearts He had made for Himself longed for a God who could be seen and heard and touched, a God to whom they could draw near with their offerings of praise and thanksgiving, and above all, of propitiation. The widespread prevalence of idolatry testifies to the universality of this desire, and among the chosen people we hear such cries as: "Who will give Thee to me for my Brother?"[1] "Drop down dew, ye heavens from above, and let the clouds rain the Just; let the earth be opened and bud forth a Saviour."[2] "Oh that Thou wouldst rend the Heavens and come down!"[3]

Four thousand years of that mysterious yearning for Him—and then He came. "Afterwards He was seen upon earth and conversed with men."[4]

He came amongst us as one of ourselves. He placed Himself completely at our disposal, to lead the kind of life, to die the sort of death that should be most helpful to us. Men passed Him in the streets, jostled Him in the crowd, watched Him at prayer, sat by Him at meat, approved or criticised His dealings with the sick, the lowly, the sorrowful, the sin-stained. So attractive, that thousands, bearing their sick with them, flocked into the desert or toiled up the mountains after Him, unmindful of hunger, shelter, the necessary pursuits of life, if only from daybreak to sundown they might look upon His Face; so mighty, that disease and death, and the devils themselves obeyed Him; that the ministers sent to apprehend Him, paralysed and then fascinated, went away saying: "Never did man

---

1   Cant. 8:1.   2   Isaias 45:8.   3   Isaias 64:1.
4   Baruch 3:38.

speak like this Man"[1]; so gentle, that the little children played about Him and nestled on His breast; infinitely refined, yet content in the society of the simple and the uncouth; of exquisite sensibility, yet uncomplaining amid the fiercest tortures of body and mind; faithful to His friends, merciful to His enemies, grateful for kindness, easily moved to tears—so He lived amongst us for three and thirty years!

And so he remains amongst us still. This it is, that is so hard to realise in a way that makes His Presence a real and constant influence on our lives. His character as revealed to us in the Gospels, attracts us; we envy the multitudes that thronged Him, and long to have come ourselves under His charm. But we do not throng His churches, nor by frequent visits and the daily Communion now brought within our reach, seek familiar intercourse with Him. We say in excuse that the absence of all sensible evidence of His Presence destroys any parallel between ourselves and the eager Jewish crowds.

It would be foolish to deny the force of this objection. Yet the Saints did not argue thus, or allow themselves to be disconcerted because the Providence of God had not thought fit to place their time of trial nineteen centuries back, and their home in Galilee or Judea. By acts of faith, and by living up to their faith, Jesus on the Altar became to them what Jesus of Nazareth was to the Jewish multitudes of His day. They knew Him to be the same "yesterday, today and for ever,"[2] and hastened to Him with every need. They brought Him their adoration like the shepherds of

1   John 7:46.   2   Heb. 13:8.

Bethlehem and the Twelve on the hushed Lake and the five hundred on the Mount of the Ascension. They brought Him their anxious questionings like Nicodemus, their little children like the Jewish mothers, their broken hearts like the sisters of Bethany, their sins like Magdalen.

It was an effort that cost at first, for the imagination and the restless senses crave something on which to fasten. But they persevered, and found, as we may find, that faith is able to bear the burden put upon it during this life of trial. *Sola fides sufficit,* the Church persists in saying to her children of each generation. And she proves it age after age by the Saints whose heroic faith is continually raising them to her altars.

Why must we have at once, and without price, what others have toiled for perseveringly and at great cost? Why not rather say: "I earnestly desire the end, therefore I will take the means?" It is the Presence of Jesus in her midst that makes all the difference between the Church of Christ and her counterfeits. It is the fuller realisation of that Presence to which we can all attain, that brings at last the glad acknowledgement that His tabernacles *are* lovely;[1] that the Lord hidden there is indeed sweet;[2] that the vigorous exercise of our faith, and patient prayer, are after all but a small price to pay for that experimental knowledge of God which is the happiness of this life, and a foretaste of the possession of God which makes the beatitude of eternity.

---

1   Ps. 83:2.   2   Ps. 33:9.

XXIII

EVENTIDE

"Stay with us because it is towards evening." (Luke 24:29.)

AMONG the experiences of later life is the sense of loneliness that deepens as we near the end of our journey. We account for it by the fact that we have outlived our generation, our interests, our work in life, and by the disappearance from our path of so many who started with us, and whose presence and friendship were for long our support in the way.

But there is more than this. The sense of isolation which grows upon us is the foreshadowing of the hour when we must go down into the dark valley alone. It is thus a grace of detachment which belongs to the later years of life.

The word "detachment" has a mournful sound for us. It speaks of the severance of strong and tender ties, and of the anguish and desolation that follow. This is one aspect of it. But to faith—and it is now we find the support and consolation our faith is to us—detachment has a brighter side. By making room in our hearts for God, it is a preparation for a closer attachment to Him who is soon to be to us All in All. God never takes but to make good the loss. If He loosens our hold on the things of earth, it is because the time is coming when we shall want to fasten our whole grasp on Him who can alone avail us when all else falls away.

He leads us to lean on Him more and more. We find Him quietly taking possession of the vacant places in our hearts, and training us to count on His friendship and sympathy as that of earth fails us. He does not mean us to live on with empty hearts, or to steel ourselves against the need of affection, but only—and more completely as the friends of this life disappear—to depend on Him who gave them to us, who set their path beside our own, and made them what they were to us, that in their love and faithfulness we might see some faint reflection of His.

He wants us more and more to Himself now. It is not only because eye and hand and brain are less apt for their tasks that He transfers these to others, but because we are nearing the time when the things of eternity will take the place of business here, and it behooves us to be preparing for it. As the work of this world falls from our hands, we must take up that which is to be our occupation for ever. St. Bernard says somewhere that when two things are to be joined together, the ends must correspond. What we want our future life to be, we must take care the end of this life shall be.

It is hard for us to realise existence apart from the things of sense which hem us in here on every side. We have to be weaned from them by degrees that we may learn to centre our affections on God and hold Him in place of all things else.

"My God and my All!" Let us try to savour these words. In our quiet, solitary hours—and there will be more of these now—we should turn our thoughts Heavenwards, and, as St. Paul bids us,[1] have our conversation there. A princess who is to take her place shortly in a foreign Court, begins to learn the language of the country and to familiarise herself with its ways; so must we in the later years of life. Thus shall we come to see things from the true standpoint and to appraise the affairs of this passing world at their right value.

If the sense of failing strength, helplessness and uselessness depresses us, let us look forward to the new life, the renewed energy, the abundant scope for the exercise of all the faculties that will be ours before long.

What matter if the world begins to look like a strange place, with the old landmarks gone, the old places untenanted! We have "a lasting city"[2] "an eternal habitation,"[3] awaiting us.

If every hour and on every side we miss the dear familiar faces of other days, let us look for them where Angels see them now, where we shall see them again—before the Throne of God.

And if at times we look back wistfully to the home of the past, let us rouse our faith to look forward longingly to the home restored in Heaven, which each bereavement here on earth is perfecting, and where the joy of reunion will exceed all expectation and desire.

But it is God Himself whom we are to desire before and above all things in eternity. To each and every one of the Blessed He is simply everything. "Our God"[4] is the

---

1   Philip. 3:20.   2   Heb. 13:14.   3   2 Cor. 5:1.
4   Apoc. 7:3.

name which expresses at once their love of Him, their delight in the possession of Him, their joy that all in that vast family have found in Him their all-sufficing good. "My God and my All!" is the rapturous, untiring cry of each. All else is but the overflow of their happiness, utterly insignificant when set beside that possession of Him which is their essential beatitude. How anything can be put in competition with Him, how they could ever have preferred their pleasure to His, is incomprehensible to them now. His Will, His preferences, His Glory, the least act, desire, or thought that concerns His interests or service, they make much account of, the rest is nothing to them.

So will it be with us the moment life is passed. It will be so by the necessity of the eternal realities into which we enter when these transitory things come to an end. They are given to us as instruments during our probation with which to work out our salvation. In themselves they have no value. Health, sickness, wealth, poverty, success, failure—all these from that height are seen in their true light, as things to be desired or shunned only in so far as they help or hinder us Heavenwards.

This will be clear to us as the daylight now. There will be no merit in the sight, nor will it affect our lot in eternity. But to adjust our views *now* to the standpoint there, to look here at the things of time as they are seen there, to hold pleasant things with a loose hand, and to take hard things cheerfully as means of laying up spiritual treasure—this will make a marvellous difference to our nearness to God and therefore to our happiness throughout eternity.

"We must be getting every way,"[1] now that the time is short, and heap up treasure every moment by a good use of the chances and so-called mischances of life. And this is easier than heretofore. The fascinations that once bewitched us have long since loosed their hold; eternal things as we near them come out in their true proportions; the mist on the distant hills is lifting, and there is little to make us tarry on the way. We must think less of remaining trials than of the work they are doing for us. The end of the journey is too near now for overmuch sorrow at the troubles of the close: "When these things begin to come to pass, look up and lift up your heads, because your redemption is at hand."[2]

The young are said to live in the future, the old in the past. If it be so, let us see that the retrospect be one of thankfulness and praise, not a morbid harbouring of vain regrets. But, we too, must live in the Future. Who should do so if not those who in the near distance see the gates of their Home! We must think more of what will be in a few years at most than of what was once. Is it not a poor return to make for the Kingdom prepared for us from the beginning of the world, that we see its approach with resignation only; that we never say from our hearts: "Thy Kingdom come," or with the longing heart of St. Paul: "I desire to be dissolved and to be with Christ"? Has the old world of sin and trouble which is slipping away from beneath our feet, more hold on our hearts than the world of spotless sanctity and joy which we are entering?

The Blessed will tell us with loving reproach that we have never yet known true joy; that the exchange of this world for the next is the exchange of death for life; that this

1   Wisd. 15:12.   2   Luke 21:28.

new life is freedom, expansion, peace, absolute content, gain every way. God's promises are magnificent, and one and all there bear Him testimony: "There has not so much as one thing failed of all He promised."[1]

Let the things of this world go, then. We must loose the ropes, and lift the gangway, and push off from one shore before we can reach the other. Let us keep our faces Heavenwards, and our heart with our Treasure there.

If we can unite ourselves more frequently, even daily, with Our Lord in Holy Communion, this will be the best preparation for the face to face union that is at hand. Every time we receive Him, every aspiration of love as the hours of the day go by, and in our waking hours at night, wins for us new nearness to Him for ever.

And we shall want Him near us before we come to Him within the veil. He alone can go down with us into the dark valley of the shadow of death; His arm alone can uphold us when all things of this world fall away. Only His Voice can comfort and His Presence protect us in the perils of that hour. What He will be to us then, and through the eternity that is to follow, will depend very much on what He is to us at present.

Therefore now at eventide, when the shadows lengthen and remind us that our day's work here is nearly done, we must entreat and constrain Him, saying: "It is towards evening and the day is now far spent, abide with us, abide with us, O Lord!"

---

1   3 Kings 8:56.

XXIV

IN THE STORM

VERY life has its crucial points. Sometimes we see them from afar and have time for preparation; sometimes, turning a corner, we come upon them unawares. Often they seem to thrust themselves upon us as obstacles in our way when in reality they are golden opportunities to be seized and utilised to the full. Our future here and hereafter may be decided by them. Yet without vigilance and courage to recognise them for what they are, we may either pass them by heedlessly or come into collision with them to our cost.

> There is a tide in the affairs of men,
> Which, taken at the flood, leads on to fortune;
> Omitted, all the voyage of our life
> Is bound in shallows and in miseries
> And we must take the current when it serves,
> Or lose our ventures.[1]

These epoch-making crises often come in the shape of a trial that taxes the resources and calls for all the energy of the soul to meet the pressure put upon it and to correspond with the grace that is offered. It may be

---

1   *Julius Caesar.*

the death of one whose life through happy years has been one with our own. It may be the failure of an enterprise on which our hopes were set, the loss of fortune, position, influence, health. What we had thought part of ourselves has suddenly gone from us, and life has become a blank.

The blow stuns at first; only by degrees do we realise its full force—and then comes the question: Shall we call to our help the succours of Faith, or shall we fling ourselves passionately on the grave of our treasure, reject all that would bring us consolation and strength, harden ourselves against the trial and Him who sends it, sink down into selfish despondency, and thus not only frustrate the designs of God, but turn into matter for chastisement what was sent in love?

Which will it be? Much depends on our habit of mind in the past. If the sense of the sovereignty of God's Will has penetrated us through and through, and trust in the wisdom and tenderness of that Will is part of our very selves, it will be well with us now; the spirit of reverence and submissiveness in which our soul is steeped will stand us in good stead: "the rain fell and the floods came and the winds blew and they beat upon that house and it fell not, for it was founded upon a rock."[1]

But suppose there has been no such habit formed in the past, no such preparation provided against the day of trial—what will help us in a time of peril like this when submission to God and trust in God seem to be failing us?

If we have not these deep-seated convictions of Faith to fall back upon, we must rely all the more absolutely on

1   Matth. 7:25.

the actual grace which will not be wanting. Enough grace to resist the strongest temptation, God always gives; more than enough—abundant, superabundant—will be given in proportion to the earnestness with which we have recourse to Him in prayer.

But we cannot, we say, make the effort to pray; the sense of rebellion is too strong for us and stifles the words on our lips; the weight that crushes us is too heavy to be thrown off; the void in our lives is too awful to face. We have misread God's dealings with us in the past; we cannot kiss His hand now nor throw ourselves into His arms. All we ask is to be left to ourselves; our friends must not beset us with considerations and consolations that have lost their force.

Courage! God was never nearer to us than now, for to the trial that came from Him, and that with His help was not too heavy for our strength, is superadded the cruel burden of temptation flung upon us by the enemy to crush and drive us to despair. Despondency is settling down upon us like the torpor of the sleeper in the snow; we must rouse ourselves. God is at hand, solicitous, ready to help. We must call upon Him as earnestly as we can: "Lord, save us, we perish!"

The effort will cost *but we can make it.* Reluctantly, perhaps, and feebly we try to bring our will into conformity with the Will of God: "Father, not my will but Thine be done"—and peace begins to steal into our soul. God has met us more than halfway. He knows the struggle and accepts the goodwill. Oh, that we could find it in our heart to give Him more than the bare submission to which we are bound! that we could make an act of faith in the wisdom and love of all His appointments; that we could delight Him with the grand act of hope which the extremity of anguish wrung from His servant Job: "The Lord gave and the Lord hath taken away, blessed be the name of the Lord;[1] though He should slay me I will trust in Him."[2]

---

1 Job 1:21.   2 Job 13:15.

XXV

MY CREATOR

REATOR—how unattainable is the idea! The mind grows giddy at the attempt to grasp it. We stand bewildered before what we are pleased to call the creations of genius, yet what are they? Only the shifting into place of the innumerable materials made available and experimented on by others, another modification of them like the combinations of the kaleidoscope; but what is this to creation?

What must He be who has not only made but *created* me? And by what names can I call the rights which the act of creation necessarily gives Him over me and all I have or can do? What are the rights entailed by fabrication or invention, rights so jealously vindicated and protected, compared with the rights my Creator has over me, the work of His hands, rights over my understanding, and memory, and will, rights as to the ordering of my thoughts, and desires, and affections and every detail of conduct throughout my life?

The difficulty here is not to understand the sovereignty of His claims, but how He is able to make His Will or good pleasure other than binding under sin; how, in consideration of my weakness, He can so far condescend as to say: "This you shall not do under pain of forfeiting My friendship; this shall constitute an offence, yet not a grievous one; and this I put before you as more acceptable to Me, you may comply with it or not without displeasing Me." Such liberality reason may find it hard to justify in theory, but oh! how different it all is when we come to the carrying out of what reason so unhesitatingly approves.

I find myself in life, with a certain equipment of gifts and faculties that necessarily suppose matter for their exercise and responsibility for their use. And my faith, corroborating and supplementing my reason, tells me that my Creator, who, by His very nature is goodness and diffusive goodness, has chosen, out of all possible creatures whom He might have preferred, to create me, to make over to me, together with my life, the faculties of soul and body and all the multiplicity of created things which I enjoy.

He was free to create or not to create me. But He was not free as to the end of my creation, nor could He so constitute my being as to make me independent of Himself. He Himself must be my End. I am to serve Him, not mediately like the irrational creatures, but directly. I am not made for any creature but for Himself. My safety, my happiness, my glory is to remain in close and willing dependence on Him and to devote to His service all He has given me. This He has a right to exact from me without attaching reward to it, but His Will is to recompense with eternal happiness not only my life as a whole, but every thought, word, and act directed to His glory and service.

Miserable shall I be if, disregarding the light that reason itself provides, and perverting the gifts I have straight from His hand, I affect independence of Him, cut myself free of Him as far as this depends on my will, live my life for myself, give Him only the service I dare not refuse Him and give Him that grudgingly; if I question His rights, and grumble at commands, sacrifice, and pain which curtail my liberty and my pleasure.

Is this the return with which reason—to say nothing of faith—would have me requite what I may truly call His labour in my service? for everything I have and use and enjoy is from Him, given with a lavishness and a love that no devotedness of mine can ever acknowledge or repay. He is obliged even in my interests to keep me in dependence on Him; out of Him there is no good for me; in this life as in the next my happiness is to carry out His plan for me. How can I be so foolish as to think I can find a better way for myself than that which my All-Wise and loving Creator has marked out for me, to which, by the very necessity of my nature, I am bound!

He who created me must surely know me better than I know myself. About every particle of my being, soul and body, He knows all there is to know. All lies before Him clear as day, without disguise or complication. The working of hereditary instincts, of early influences, of growing will-power later on; the materials that have gone to build up character; the tendencies that are making for good or for evil; coming dangers, opportunities and graces, and the incessant action of my freewill upon all this up to my last breath—He knows.

Surely He must know better than I what is necessary to fill the capacity for happiness which He has given me; and when He tells me that wealth, comfort, pleasure, honour, earthly affection, will not satisfy me because I was not made for any of these things, and that union with Him, begun now by sanctifying grace, perfected in eternity by the face to face Vision, full possession and enjoyment of Him, will alone content me—I may and must trust Him implicitly. Not by doling out my service, not by shirking sacrifice, shall I satisfy either myself or Him, but only by giving Him of my best, and deserving by eminent service that distinguished place in His Kingdom which means a clearer sight, a fuller possession of Him for ever.

My service of God would gain immeasurably were I not perpetually looking back to see if my own interests were following close in its wake. It is self-seeking that by dividing my forces hampers me at every turn. Once let there be the conviction—deep, palpable, self-evident—that His interests are mine and mine His, and the way is open to the generous devotedness that is able to do great things for God.

XXVI

"STIR UP THY MIGHT...
STIR UP OUR HEARTS, O LORD"

(Mass for the First, Second, and Fourth Sundays of Advent.)

LITTLE children spend the best part of their time asleep, and it is good for them. Is it too much to say that we, the children of the Church, spend the greater part of our lives asleep, to the utter undoing of many, to the great and irreparable loss of all?

Our Mother does all she can to rouse us, to get us to shake off our lethargy, and wake up to a sense of the thrilling realities around us on every side. Now she takes us down into the eternal prison-house, that knowing its terrors in life, we may not know them after death. Now she throws Heaven open before us, that the glory and happiness of those who have realised the meaning of life, and time, and eternity may stir us to emulation and effort. In the spring time when the green earth is teeming with beauty and with promise, she draws us aside and lays ashes on our head, and bids us remember Death. Our Lord's word of warning she would have ever in our ears:

"Watch! for you know not the day nor the hour."

But it is especially at the beginning and close of the ecclesiastical year that she strives to startle us into attention. Twice in succession she puts before us the closing scene of the world's history and the final award of happiness or misery to every member of the human race. And three times she follows up this solemn lesson by the prayer that it may not fall upon deaf ears and hearts: *Stir up thy might, stir up our hearts, O Lord.*

To stir up is not to create but to call into activity what is there already but latent. We stir the bed of thyme and it gives out its fragrance; we stir our limbs and they go forth to deeds of strength. The Omnipotence of God is at our service always, and at the instance of prayer is stirred in our behalf. But we, too, must be stirred, or His desire and His power to help will avail us nothing. His holy Spirit which in the beginning moved over the waters, must wake into activity the faith that is in us. It must be His work, for of ourselves we can do nothing. Love, fear, anger, desire, the events and interests of daily life stir us readily enough where the things of this life are concerned, but the impulse of our hearts towards any supernatural good must come from Him.

Therefore we pray Him to stir up our hearts, to rouse them from their torpor, to call into activity the faith of our baptism which only waits His touch to put its mighty forces into operation. The Saints prayed this prayer, and its answer was the heroism which throughout eternity will be the admiration of Angels and men. Their faith is ours and is ready to show its strength in our hearts as in theirs.

What is wanted is the touch that will set it in motion, and so we pray: *Stir up Thy might, stir up our hearts, O Lord.*

My God, come Thyself into my heart and stir it to its depths, that all that is within me may be alert, eager, zealous, holding itself ready for Thy service. Stir up my faith that it may be the strong, living principle it was in the souls of the Saints. Stir up my hope, to trust Thee with the unquestioning confidence Thou hast a right to expect from Thy child. Stir up my love and warm my heart by contact with Thine own. Stir up my desires that like the sluggish rivers of low-lying lands are apt to lose themselves in the things of earth around them. Stir them up to run with a strong stream to the Sea from whence they came—to Thee, O Infinite God, the Source of all my good.

XXVII

"GLORIOUS IN HOLINESS"

(Exodus 15:11.)

E ARE apt to think of God's glory as if it were something external to Himself, as if it consisted in the witness borne Him by the starry firmament, the fruitful earth, the mighty sea; in the multitude of His heavenly courtiers; the service and praise of His Church; the sanctity of His Saints; the spread of His Kingdom upon earth.

All these, indeed, declare the glory of God, but they do not constitute His essential glory, the testimony within Himself rendered to Him by His Divine Perfections, and by that one in particular which most especially declares His Essence, in whose white light all are unified—His Holiness.

In terms of rapture Moses cries: "Who is like to Thee, O Lord, glorious in holiness!"[1] And David: "They shall speak of the magnificence of the glory of Thy holiness."[2] It is the attribute which we on earth and still in probation, adore with deepest, trembling worship. Like the sun in the heavens at noonday, its dazzling glory blinds us when we

---

1   Exod. 15:11.   2   Ps. 144:5.

try to look at it, for we are sin-stained always, even at our best. From first to last we are sinners—penitent, indeed, and forgiven—yet for all that, sinners still. Failing every morning, failing seven times and more every day, how should we be able to raise our eyes to the Holiness of God!

Even when we have left behind us this body of clay, and the soul "sick with love," hastens to the embrace of its Beloved, even then love and desire are checked like Magdalen by the Holiness that is "a consuming fire."[1]

> ...Praise to His Name!
> The eager spirit has darted from my hold,
> And, with the intemperate energy of love,
> Flies to the dear feet of Emmanuel;
> But, ere it reach them, the keen sanctity,
> Which with its effluence, like a glory, clothes
> And circles round the Crucified, has seized,
> And scorched, and shrivell'd it; and now it lies
> Passive and still before the awful Throne.
> O happy suffering soul! for it is safe,
> Consumed, yet quicken'd by the glance of God.[2]

Isaias heard the Seraphim crying to one another: "Holy, Holy, Holy, the Lord God of Hosts."[3] The four living creatures seen by St. John, "rested not day and night, saying: Holy, Holy, Holy, Lord God Almighty, who was and who is and who is to come."[4] As if it was the light of that dazzling Holiness that most fascinated, enraptured and inflamed them, and inspired that cry of everlasting praise, echoed daily by the Church on earth in the Holy Mass.

The worship of this Divine Attribute, so attractive, yet so terrible, seeing we are what we are, has a special fitness in

---

1 Deut. 4:24, Heb. 12:29. 2 Newman, *The Dream of Gerontius.*
3 Isaias 6:3.   4 Apoc. 4:8.

these days. Because the Sovereignty of God is so generally ignored, the sense of reverence is well nigh lost, and the appreciation of the malice of sin, outside the Church, and to a great extent inside, is dulled to a degree unknown in earlier and healthier times.

Men talk of God nowadays as if He were merely a problem for investigation by such processes as they choose to adopt, whose existence or non-existence being decided by their verdict, the case is dismissed without appeal. If He exists, He may be allowed a certain amount of respect, but no interference with the world and its ways. His rights, His Will, His commands, His punishments—these were burdens and terrors to frighten a superstitious age. We have got beyond all that now.

Everything is open to the criticism of learned and ignorant alike; the awe of treading on holy ground is a delusion of the past; not only the revealed but the natural law is denied. Sin may be a mistake, a falling short of what we owe to ourselves, but as an offence, an injustice, an outrage to our Maker—this conception of it is being lost, and God who has their breath in His hand[1] is flouted by the creatures formed from the dust of the earth.

Is not reparation to His Holiness called for, and will it not have a special acceptance now, even when offered by such as we know ourselves to be!

> "We are not Angels, but we may
> Down in earth's corners kneel,
> And multiply sweet acts of love,
> And murmur what we feel.[2]

---

1   Dan. 5:23.   2   Father Faber.

XXVIII

"THIS IS THE WILL OF GOD CONCERNING YOU"

(1 Thess. 5:18.)

THE message brought us every hour of our life by every duty, every call for sacrifice, every glad surprise, every disappointment, every change of circumstance, every contradiction, every trouble arising from health, or weather, or the ways of those about us. "This is the Will of God," comes inscribed on every one of them; the merit of life consists in seeing the inscription and in acting up to it.

Our misfortune is that we fail to see that all these things are the Will of God. In health and sickness, and the weather, and perhaps in a clear answer to prayer, we manage to recognise the Divine Will. But as to disagreeables that come through the mistakes or the ill will of others—in these we refuse to see anything but the happenings of blind chance or the malice of men.

Theoretically we allow that there is no such thing as chance, but when trouble comes, philosophy and religion go to the winds, and the teaching that God works through human instruments for our trial and our training, we rebel against, and by our conduct practically deny.

Many who do not go to this length, who recognize that this is the Will of God even when it acts through the agency of others, think they have done all that is required of them, all that is possible to do, if they accept of visitations as their appointed fate, abstain from murmuring, at least outwardly, and sink down into a state of hopeless despondency.

"What more can I do?" they ask, "but take what cannot be helped, and bear it without rebellion?"

Oh, yes! we can do more than this, a great deal more. If we think of the claims of the Divine Will upon us, we shall see that not resignation only, but humble gratitude and childlike hopefulness which smiles through its tears, are not beyond our strength, grace aided.

Think of the Sovereignty of the Divine Will and of what It implies. What we make we look upon as altogether ours, and we resent any interference with what, by the very fact of its existence, is our absolute property. Must not at least the same amount of right be allowed to Him who is not Maker only but Creator? May He not give and take as He wills, in accordance with His eternal plan?

Think, too, of the Wisdom of this Sovereign Will. It is not as ours, capricious and blind. Its designs for us here and hereafter have been in the Mind of God eternally, as the best possible means for the attainment of the happiness for which He has created us. Do we question the wisdom of an earthly father when he subjects the child of his hopes to the discipline and training which are to fit him for his inheritance? "For what son is there whom the father does not correct?"[1]

And the Will of God is tender. This is what is hardest to acknowledge when we are smarting beneath a blow. But here again the law of earthly love holds good and ought to help us. We condemn as false and cruel the tenderness that shrinks from inflicting necessary pain. Why, then, mistrust the infinite tenderness of our Heavenly Father in our hours of trial? Though we wince and cry, He carries through His designs of merciful correction, encouraging us the while with tenderer words than ever fell from human lips:

"For a small moment have I forsaken thee, but with great mercies will I gather thee. In a moment of indignation have I hid My face a little while from thee, but with everlasting kindness have I had mercy on thee, said the Lord, thy Redeemer. O poor little one, tossed by the tempest, without all comfort, behold I will lay thy stones in order, and will lay thy foundations with sapphires...and make all thy borders of desirable stones."[2]

Shall we not abandon ourselves with trust to the Will of God, Sovereign, All-Wise, infinitely Kind? Is it return enough to make for Its plans of eternal friendliness, that we should abstain from rebellion when they bring us a passing smart? "Go with them, doubting nothing,"[3] God says to us of His messengers. We have nothing to fear from them; we may safely welcome them, and go with them, entering into the designs of God which they bring us—*doubting nothing.*

---

1 Heb. 12:7.   2 Isaias 54:7-8, 11-12.   3 Acts 10:20.

XXIX

LOVE IN CHASTISEMENT

"Such as I love I rebuke and chastise." (Apoc. 3:19.)

HOW hard it is to realise this with the strong practical conviction that has an influence upon our lives! Speculatively, and in its application to others our appreciation of it leaves nothing to be desired. In the misfortunes that befall our friends, those especially who we may well believe are among the "such as I love," we have no difficulty in seeing the hand of God chastising them and training them for the heavenly Kingdom.

But the case is different when our own turn for the training and the chastisement comes. Either we look exclusively at secondary causes and human instruments, and pursue them with our resentment and vengeance, or, if we give ear to our charitable friends who venture to suggest to us the motives for consolation with which we so readily furnished them in their hour of trial, it is only to turn away fretfully from the words of comfort as not fitting our case.

"Behold thou hast taught many and thou hast strengthened the weary hands. Thy words have confirmed them that were staggering, and thou hast strengthened the trembling knees. But now the scourge is come upon thee and thou faintest; it hath touched thee and thou art troubled. Where is thy fortitude, thy patience, and the perfection of thy ways?"[1]

More tenderly, indeed, than the exasperating friends of Job do ours press upon us motives for comfort, but, it may be, with unavailing kindness.

"True," we say, "trials are fatherly chastisements from God in the case of the Saints. It is easy enough for them to accept troubles from His hand and to profit by them, but I cannot look at things in this light. It is my unfortunate character or surroundings or, worse still, my sins past or present, my general unsatisfactoriness in the service of God that brings all this upon me."

Well, granting this—what then?

There is a startling rebuke in Scripture addressed to one who is described by God Himself much as some of us might be inclined to describe ourselves—"miserable and poor and blind and naked." "I know thy works that thou art neither hot nor cold....Because thou art lukewarm and neither hot nor cold, I will begin to vomit thee out of my mouth."[2]

Then, following close upon these terrific words, is the assurance to the trembling soul that it is loved, dearly loved in spite of its misery—and therefore warned and corrected: "Such as I love I rebuke and chastise. Be zealous, therefore, and do penance."

It is just, then, these very indifferent servants of God, with whom we rank ourselves, to whom the hard words

---

1   Job 4:3-6.   2   Apoc. 3:15-16.

and hard trials come *as proofs of love.*

Our guides in the spiritual life tell us that whenever reflection upon sin past or present has a depressing effect upon us, lessens our trust in God, and leaves our soul limp and spiritless, we may take it for granted that it is not the work of the Spirit of God but the product of Satan's malice and of our own self-love. He is perpetually suggesting to us that God is angry with us, that we have deserved all this, and so on. An easy but disconcerting answer is to admit cheerfully all that he alleges.

"We indeed, justly," said the poor thief amid the terrible onslaughts of despair and death. It was the humble avowal of the sins of a lifetime and an acceptance of all the punishment they had merited. But he did not stop there. Enlightened by grace, he went on to make reparation by a most glorious confession of the Divinity of his fellow Sufferer, and to trust himself entirely to His remembrance and mercy. Let us follow his example.

"You have brought this punishment on yourself," whispers the tempter. "There was that unkind story with which you entertained your visitors yesterday; and sloth in rising this morning; and the angry retort just now, all the worse because you had just come from Mass and Communion."

"Quite true," we reply, "and well put. I am glad to have these things recalled to mind. And I am sorry for them, and humble myself before God for them, and with His help will be more careful in future. And now, what next?"

If this is difficult, and we feel the waves of discouragement tossing and filling the boat, we must bale them out briskly or they will sink us. No matter what right they can show to be there, they must be got rid of at once or it will be all over with us. If every hour of the day we had fallen into grievous sin, all the more need would there be for a resolute stand against despondency. And if disaster such as this will not warrant it, how much less will the seven falls which is the daily experience of even the just man.

It is not so much the falls as the discouragement which follows them, out of which the devil is prepared to make capital. If we rise at once, and with an act of humble sorrow and fresh trust throw ourselves anew upon God: "Lord, remember me. I have sinned, but I am sorry," and do this again and again as often as we fall, we shall not only recover our ground, but little by little make headway and reach the goal at last.

It is a poor argument, then, against trial being a loving chastisement in our case, to say that we are among the commonplace and faulty servants of God. It is precisely these whom He calls: "such as I love," and who, after the Father's chastisement, may look for the Father's embrace—and reward.

XXX

"OPEN TO ME"

(Cant. 5)

"If any man open to Me the door, I will come in to him and will sup with him and he with Me." (Apoc. 3:20.)

"I was a stranger and you took me in." (Matth. 25:35.)

OW charming is the Divine courtesy of these words! bearing no faintest shade of the condescension that honours with a visit, but only the solicitations of a friend, or the humble gratitude of a guest. "You took Me in." As if He were beholden to us for shelter and sympathy and kindness, and would let us know His appreciation of it all.

As if—we say. But there can be no make-believe in the very Truth. His courtesy can never be what ours too often is, mere simulation of kindness. When He says: "My delights are to be with the children of men,"[1] we must take the sweet words literally, and store them away in memory and heart among the other mysteries of His incomprehensible charity.

---

1 Prov. 8:31.

He does love to be with us; the proofs are too numerous and incontestable to be called in question. Infinite distance was not too far to travel when the Word was made flesh and dwelt amongst us. And, once in our midst, how completely He made Himself at home! Not, indeed, by surrounding Himself with what men covet—His foothold on earth, a manger for a cradle, a cross for a deathbed, was as scant as even Omnipotence could make it—but by sharing our joys and our sorrows, though in unequal measure, thereby to establish with us that fellowship of interests which only the experience of life's ups and downs can bring about.

He loves to be with us, and does not hesitate to show His satisfaction. See the readiness with which during His Public Life He accepted hospitality, not only when it was genuine as at Cana but when its character was more than doubtful as in the house of the Pharisee. Twice at least He was the Guest of that despised and detested class, the publicans. "And it came to pass as He was sitting at meat in the house, behold many publicans and sinners came and sat down with Jesus and His disciples."

What a spectacle for the Holy Angels was that feast in the house of Matthew! the Lord before whom they cover their faces with their wings and sing continually: "Holy, Holy, Holy," in the midst of "extortioners, unjust," notorious sinners, not overawing them by His presence but attracting and charming them by the graciousness of His conversation and ways.

We may note in passing how often the homely time of "sitting at meat" was chosen by Him both before and after the Resurrection for some of His sweetest words to us. When the Pharisees in Matthew's house took scandal at the familiarity of the Master with such disreputable companions, He said: "they that are in health need not the physician but they that are sick....I am not come to call the just but sinners."[1] When, as he entered the house of Zaccheus, who "received Him with joy, all murmured saying He was gone to be the guest of a man that was a sinner, He answered: The Son of Man is come to seek and to save that which was lost." And when, as He sat at meat in the house of the Pharisee, Magdalen came and anointed and kissed His feet, He said in her defence: "Many sins are forgiven her because she hath loved much...thy sins are forgiven thee, go in peace." Her twice repeated act of hospitality is one of the incidents recorded by all the Evangelists, a fulfillment of His grateful promise that wherever the Gospel should be preached it should be told in remembrance of her.

Wherever our Lord was received on earth, He left signs of the acceptableness to Him of the invitation. Nay, He anticipated invitation and invited Himself: "Zaccheus, make haste and come down for this day I must abide in thy house." No sooner has the centurion mentioned his sick servant than there is the prompt answer: "I will come and heal him."[2]

How keenly, then, His sensitive Heart must have felt coldness and neglect. What He must have suffered in those last days of His preaching and miracles when nightfall brought no friendly offer of shelter and hospitality: when, uninvited to any of the homes He had made so glad, He

---

1   Matth. 9:12-13.   2   Matth. 8:7.

left the City, and took His way wearily over Olivet, to seek in the little household of Bethany where He was always welcome, the kindness denied Him in Jerusalem.

Yes, He loves to be with us. Once only do we find Him declining, or seeming to decline an invitation. At the door of the little inn at Emmaus "He made as though He would go further" and the disciples had to use a gentle violence to detain Him. "Stay with us," they said, "for it is towards evening and the day is now far spent." What wonder they did not recognise in the stranger who had to be constrained, the Master who so gladly accepted hospitality "all the time," says St. Peter, "that the Lord Jesus came in and went out amongst us."[1]

There was no real unwillingness; it was but a device of love, one of those playfulnesses of His Risen Life which reveal to us a new side in the human beauty of His divinely beautiful character, one of those acts by which He restrained for an instant the eagerness of His Sacred Heart for Its fuller flow of loving-kindness to Its beloved.

He is the same now; His delights are still to be with us; let us receive Him joyfully in whatever guise He presents Himself.

"Behold, I stand at the door and knock."[2] Who would not open to Him gladly if through the casement were seen the halo round His Head or the wounded Hands and Feet! But the praise and reward when He comes again in His glory are for the faith that knew and welcomed Him when He came to it in disguise. "I was a Stranger—and you took Me in." He comes to us in many an unexpected garb; we

1 Acts 1:21.   2 Apoc. 3:20.

have to learn to see Him in His representatives—in the inquirer whom we may help to a knowledge of Catholic truth; in the young girl who needs friendly interest and sympathy to enable her to withstand the difficulties or dangers of her surroundings; in the child who cries to us for the shelter and training of a Catholic Home where its faith will be saved and its feet set on the way to Heaven.

How often and under what varied forms the Divine Stranger presents Himself to us! Let us be on the alert to recognise Him. Often, as heretofore, "there is no beauty in Him nor comeliness...that we should be desirous of Him....His look as it were hidden and despised, whereupon we esteemed Him not."[1] But Faith and Love are quick to see Him beneath any disguise, and cry out with St. John: "It is the Lord!"[2]

"Let the charity of the brotherhood abide in you," says St. Paul...."And hospitality do not forget, for by this some, being unawares, have entertained Angels."[3] Happy we, if we discover one day that we have entertained the Lord of Angels unawares, happy to hear from His lips: "I was a Stranger and you took Me in....Come, blessed of My Father!"

---

1 Isaias 53:2-3.　　2 John 21:7.　　3 Heb. 13:2.

XXXI

"THE SON OF MAN"

S THIS His fittest title of whom it was said at His coming into the world: "Let all the Angels of God adore Him"?[1] Is He not "God of God, Light of Light, very God of very God," "the brightness of His glory and the figure of His substance, whom He hath appointed heir of all things, by whom also He made the world"?[2]

Yes "upon His head are many diadems, and He hath a name which no man knoweth but Himself...and His name is called, THE WORD OF GOD."[3] But his own Name for Himself, His Name of predilection, the Name which is to us the fullest revelation of His character, is "the Son of Man." It is dear to Him above others because more than any other it brings Him into the midst of the human family, makes Him one of us, entitled to share with us the experiences of life, to have His part in its interests, its work, its joys and sorrows and failures and triumphs, its home affections and its friendships, its pains of body and mind.

---

1   Heb. 1:6.   2   Heb. 1:2-3.   3   Apoc. 19:12-13.

As Son of Man, He knows all these in a new way, the way of experience, a way that brings Him into touch with us as nothing else could do. It is the way that Love seeks at any cost. Union with the Beloved is its first need, to satisfy which it will break through all barriers, run all risks, endure all labour and anguish. What a distance from Heaven to earth, from the throne of His glory to the Altar and the Communion rail! Love counts it as nothing, and were there further depths to which it might descend to bring about a more intimate union with us, it would not shrink from them.

As Son of Man, He has the strongest of claims upon our allegiance, our sympathy, our confidence, and our love. For as Man He is the Head of our race, our King and Leader, our Elder Brother. We must be proud of Him, we must follow Him, we must lean on Him, and by His hands pass to the Father our poor service of adoration, praise and thanksgiving, of propitiation and petition. "By whom the Angels praise Thy Majesty,"[1] how much more His lowly human brethren! "Through Him and with Him, and in Him," says the Church again, "is to Thee, God the Father Almighty, in the unity of the Holy Ghost, all honour and glory."

As our King, the most devoted loyalty is due to Him. Not only His commands but His preferences should be law to us. His enemies, His friends, His interests should be ours; whatever belongs to His service concerns us intimately and should find us ready for personal labour and sacrifice.

As our Elder Brother, He claims our deepest and most reverent affection, and absolute trust. Through Him the

---

1   Preface of the Mass

rights of sonship are ours. He takes us by the hand and leads us to the Father. "My Father, and your Father, My God and your God."[1] All that He can communicate of the prerogatives which are His by Nature, He shares with us, the adopted children of God. For this is no empty title. St. John in his first Epistle, St. Paul in his Epistles to Romans, Galatians, and Ephesians, speak in exultation of the reality of this adoption! "Dearly beloved, we are now the sons of God....Behold what manner of charity the Father hath bestowed upon us, that we should be called and should be the sons of God."[2] "They shall be called the sons of the living God,"[3] "for you are all the children of God by faith in Christ Jesus,"[4] "and if sons, heirs also."[5] "And because you are sons, God hath sent the Spirit of His Son into your hearts, crying: 'Abba, Father!'"[6]

Not till we take our place in the Court of Heaven, our Father's House, and know by experience "the glory of the children of God,"[7] shall we grasp at all adequately the significance of those words which the Church never wearies of repeating: *Through Jesus Christ our Lord.*

Then at last we shall understand what the Son of Man is to us. How completely He has "blotted out the handwriting that was against us."[8] How he has more than repaired our losses, and the havoc made by sin; raised our nature incomparably higher than the height from which it fell, and so reinstated us in our right to the heavenly inheritance that we enter His Kingdom as children, not as servants or strangers. How He is not only Redeemer

1	John 20:17.	2	1 John 3:1-2.	3	Rom. 9:26.
4	Galat. 3:26.	5	Rom. 8:17.	6	Galat. 4:6.
7	Rom. 8:21.	8	Coloss. 2:14.		

*"When Jesus therefore had seen his mother
and the disciple standing whom he loved, he saith to his mother:
Woman, behold thy son."* (John 19:26.)

and Saviour in the past to the whole human race, but an Advocate this hour in Heaven for us one by one, "ever living to make intercession for us."[1] How He is to every one of us the Source of all good actual and to come, our reconciliation, our peace, our consolation in trial, our strength in temptation, our victory, our reward. It is His life flowing into us in our Communions that gives dignity and value to our life, and merit to our least actions, and suffering, and prayer. As "most dear children"[2] we may confidently lift our little offerings to our Father in Heaven, and be sure of his acceptance of them—*through Jesus Christ our Lord.* For His sake we may come with confidence to the Throne of Grace with our troubles and our needs. For His merits we are heard and helped, for "how hath He not with Him given us all things?"[3] It is as His members, united to Him by charity, that we are to share His glory in eternity.

Through Jesus Christ our Lord. To dwell for an instant on these words from time to time as we conclude our prayer, in order to recall what Jesus is to our human race, and personally to each of us one by one—might not this be accepted as a reparation for wandering thoughts and coldness, and be a token of gratitude and love His Heart would welcome?

---

1   Heb. 7:25.   2   Ephes. 5:1.   3   Rom. 8:32.

XXXII

"THESE THREE"

"Now there remain faith, hope, and charity, these three."
(1 Cor. 13:13.)

HEN we come to Petition in our thanksgiving after Communion, it may happen that we are so absorbed by some pressing need, spiritual or temporal, that there is no question as to what we shall ask. An obstinate temptation besets us and we take it to our Lord for His aid to overcome it. Or we want light in face of an important step, e.g., a life's choice to be made, advice to be given as to the career of another, and the like. Or, stunned by a sudden blow or loss, we crouch at His feet, and without word or prayer lay our heart in its agony before Him for His pity and His help.

But when the sense of a special need does not press, we may, unless we are on our guard, neglect Petition altogether, to our very great loss. Might it not be well to have some standing request always ready?

There are three virtues for which the Church is always praying, the acts of which are from time to time binding on us; they enter into the preparation for every Sacrament;

they should spring to our lips in time of temptation; they are to be our safeguard in the hour of death. "There remain faith, hope, and charity, these three," says St. Paul, thus singling them out for special attention; "these three" which would make all the difference in our lives if they came to be the spring of our thoughts and words and acts; "these three" which, possessed in an eminent degree, constitute sanctity.

St. Paul[1] gives a magnificent litany of the achievements of Faith, following up the praise it received from the lips of Christ Himself. It was the condition required by our Lord when the blind, the deaf, the possessed were to be healed, or the dead to be raised to life: "If thou canst believe, all things are possible to them that believe."[2] "Did I not say to thee that if thou believe thou shalt see the glory of God?"[3] "And He wrought not many miracles there because of their unbelief."[4]

Unbelief is the chief fault He reprehends in His disciples: "Where is your faith?"[5] "Why are you fearful, O ye of little faith!"[6] "O thou of little faith, why didst thou doubt?"[7]

On the other hand, the faith of those who were not of His sheep drew from Him a cry of admiration: "O woman, great is thy faith!"[8] "I have not found so great faith in Israel."[9] He tells us that if we have faith we shall remove mountains. "All things whatsoever you shall ask in prayer believing, you shall receive."[10]

---

1 Heb. 11.	2 Mark 9:22.	3 John 11:40.
4 Matth. 13:58.	5 Luke 8:25.	6 Matth. 8:26.
7 Matth. 14:31.	8 Matth. 15:28.	9 Matth. 8:10.
10 Matth. 21:22.		

Well might the Twelve who were with Him day by day and saw the wonders wrought by faith, and heard His delighted praise of it, cry out to Him: "Lord, increase our faith!"[1] Well may we who have Him as our Guest when we will, make with earnestness and persistence the same prayer. Often in preparation for Communion we seek to excite our devotion, and fail; if we tried to increase our faith we should succeed better, for faith brings devotion after it as the needle draws the thread.

Hope springs straight from faith, depends absolutely on it, and is so like it that it is hard at times to distinguish them. As an imperative duty laid on every one of us, on every prodigal no matter how far he has strayed from His Father's home, Hope is a marvellous revelation of the character of God. That we should have been allowed to hope would have been much, seeing what we have been and what we are; but to be commanded under a penalty— is not this holding the prize low down within our reach, that we may run with the more eagerness and assurance? No number of sins, however grave, no relapses, however frequent and unblushing, are any excuse in His eyes for a diminution of our Hope. What the most enduring of our friends would resent, He exacts. We must return to Him each time with the same trust, and with full confidence that we shall be forgiven. Miserable as we know our service to be, we are to look to Him with absolute reliance on His mercy for all needful grace, for perseverance, for our crown at last. O God, what must Thou be in Thyself, to treat us with goodness such as this!

---

1   Luke 17:5.

Charity will be strong if Hope is strong. To love Him for Himself who shows Himself so worthy of all love, is a sweet and easy task. As Faith and Hope blend so as to be at times indistinguishable, so does Hope melt into Love, real love that shows itself "not in word and in tongue but in deed and in truth;"[1] in self-sacrifice; in the joyful service of others for His sake; in concern for all that regards His glory. When this Love is gained, all is gained; all the dangers and difficulties of the spiritual life can be easily overcome; all the heights of sanctity are within its reach. "Love, and do what you will," the Saints tell us, for "Love is swift, strong, faithful, circumspect, long-suffering, courageous. It feels no burden, values no labour, would willingly do more than it can, complains not of impossibility because it conceives that it may and can do all things."[2]

These three—what a difference the possession of them in an eminent degree would make in our lives! Can we do better than ask with earnestness and perseverance when the Giver of all grace is with us as our Guest?

---

1 1 John 3:18.   2 *Imit.*, Bk. 3, Ch. 5.

XXXIII

DETAILS

HESE it is which give vividness and interest to a picture, a description, a narrative; which lay hold on the imagination and sink into the memory. It is in the elaboration and perfection of detail that professional work scores above that of the amateur, that all excellent results are attained in every department of labour—mechanical, artistic, literary, scientific.

And spiritual. If we want to improve the general character of our service of God, we must improve the details—our prayers, morning and night, and each of these again in detail; the fervour with which I offer to God the work of the day in my morning prayer; the honesty of my self-examination at night; in my confessions my care to make a good act of contrition and purpose of amendment; in my Communions, earnestness in the usual acts of preparation and thanksgiving, possibly, too, in my resolution not to stay away through sloth, coldness, the fear of what more frequent Communion might entail. In the way I hear Mass. Is it daily Mass? If not, why not? My remembrance of the four ends for which the Holy Sacrifice is offered—Adoration, Thanksgiving, Propitiation, Petition—my prayer for the living and the dead, my reasonable care to guard against distractions— what about all these?

So also in my relations with my neighbours; I must go into detail. Do I often think how I can make others happy? Often examine my conversations and their results? Have I a horror of rash judgments and mischief-making? Am I ingenious in finding a good word for the absent? Am I faithful in keeping secrets of trust? Am I fond of gossip and given to encourage it in others? Do I encourage detraction by inquisitiveness? Do I ever let children hear uncharitable talk, or conversation calculated to lessen their respect for those they are bound to revere? Am I patient and courteous with daily companions and ready to make sacrifices for the sake of peace? Do I pray for charity towards those against whom I feel ill will or who annoy or oppose me? Am I too exacting, unwilling to allow for mistakes or misunderstanding? Do I exercise self-control when I feel hurt and inclined to make an angry reply? Do I try to look at the best side of those I dislike? Do I think more of what I suffer from others than of what others suffer from me? Do I try to comfort those in trouble? What do I set apart for the poor?

And so again in my own spiritual advancement. If I find selfishness at the root of all or most of my misdeeds, and such a discovery is quite possible, I must make an object lesson of this ugly monster as it shows itself in the details of my life. Does it habitually make me fail in the imperative duty of rising promptly at the appointed time?

Is the secret of my infrequent Communions the trouble of going oftener, or the obligation it might bring of sacrificing this or that friendship, or dangerous self-indulgence? Do I neglect prayer because of its difficulties and the restraint it imposes? Does selfishness show itself in my neglect of duties for which I am responsible at home or elsewhere, or in carelessness as to the irksome details of my work, in the absence of anything like hard work in my life, the preponderance of pleasure over work, or in idleness or extravagance?

If candour compels me to believe that humility is what is wanted in my thoughts, words, and general conduct, I must again go into detail in my purpose of amendment. To say: "Ah, yes, very true, that is my need, and henceforth I will be proud in nothing and humble in everything," is no resolution at all but a mere velleity. But to say and to resolve, "I will turn to the thought of my sins when tempted to vanity; I will check a censorious spirit of criticism quite unbecoming in such a one as I; I will try to take slights patiently, and refrain from insisting on my own opinion, remembering how often my judgement has led me astray; I will humble myself before God whenever I kneel down to pray"—resolutions such as these, if persevered in, will certainly bring about the needed change.

To return to the subject of prayer.

Here, above all, we are apt to overlook the importance of detail. If we take for the subject of our meditation the Passion as a whole, we shall find it far too vast to grasp. It will not appeal to us or help us to appreciate what that suffering must have been and what our return of love should be, nearly so effectually as to take one point at a time and dwell on that, studying its details and giving each time to impress mind, imagination, and heart.

Have we ever thought, as we looked at a crucifix, of the pain of the scourging still fresh, and renewed by the rough dragging of the Sacred Body over the hard wood? Yet this, one only of the many terrible details, did not escape the loving mindfulness of a little child who looked pityingly, as he sat on his mother's lap, at the crucifix she held before him, and laid his finger thoughtfully and tenderly on the wounds in hands and feet. Suddenly he exclaimed: "And, mother, shan't we be sorry, too, for the pain in His poor back?"

It is details in meditation, and details, too, in our vocal prayers that make them a reality and therefore a spiritual force. Just as one suffering on the cross, the disjointing of the limbs, the hanging on the wounds, the thirst, will help us to our act of contrition before confession more efficaciously than a wider range of subject, and as to take one word at a time of a vocal prayer and dwell upon it, impresses us more and improves indefinitely the saying of that prayer in future, so will the same attention to detail help to better those Acts of Faith, Hope, Charity, Contrition, Humility, and Desire, which form so large a portion of the Church's public prayer and of our preparation for the Sacraments.

To the thousands who watch the aeroplanes soar aloft and steer their way through the air with the directness and speed of an express train, the marvel is how the bird men can keep up like that, so steadily and so long. And we wonder at the prolonged prayer of the Saints, at their hours and hours of converse with God. No doubt they had that gift of prayer which made this possible; but, no doubt, too, they won that gift by prayer, by their own persevering effort, for here as everywhere, God helps those who help themselves.

"But how," some may say, "can we make more out of Acts of Faith, Hope, and Charity than we find in our books? 'My God, I firmly believe all that Thou hast revealed and Thy Church proposes to my belief'—that is all there is to be said about it."

Not quite all. Suppose I am going to Communion and happen to have some trouble or anxiety on my mind, I may add: "I believe most firmly that Thou art coming to me today, the same Jesus of Nazareth who wast so full of tender sympathy for all in trouble. I believe that my distress will touch Thy Sacred Heart, for Thou art not changed, dear Lord, since the days of Thy life on earth." Here Faith, as is its wont, has melted into Hope, and will easily melt into Charity. "I love and thank Thee for coming to me today in my anxiety and pain, to counsel, help, and strengthen me, and do for me and mine as Thou knowest is best. My God, I know that all that happens to me is either directly sent or permitted by Thee. The act, then, that has hurt me so, was allowed by Thee as a little trial since I must have trial and am not strong enough for harder ones. I wish I had remembered this and borne it better when the pain was fresh and the merit to be had, most. Help me to see my opportunities quickly and to profit by them to the full. Let me follow Thy counsel to Thy beloved St. Catherine— accept daily trials at once and generously from Thy Hand,

and then turn my mind from them; so shall I keep my soul in peace."

In this way prayer becomes what it is meant to be—not an act of official service, formal, and brief—but a continual turning to God as to an ever-present Friend with the needs and sorrows and shortcomings of the hour, and with the trust that such recourse betokens and begets.

XXXIV

"WHAT WILT THOU
THAT I DO FOR THEE?"

(Thanksgiving after Communion)

O TWO of us make it alike, and that is best for us which keeps us most closely united with our Divine Guest during the precious time He is with us.

The first Acts with all of us will be Adoration, Thanksgiving, and Love, and, not content with our own poor efforts, many of us will call for help upon those who see Him face to face. We may offer Him the Adoration, Thanksgiving and Love of His blessed Mother, of the holy Angels, of the Saints most devoted to the Hidden God.

Or we may offer Him in compensation for our poor distracted thanksgiving now, that which without effort on our part will endure throughout eternity, impetuous, irrepressible, as that of our first hour in Heaven, employing every power of our soul in its immensely increased capacity and strength, the reward of the poor and often difficult thanksgivings of earth.

If we like, we may lead up to our Lord as His vassals, to pay Him homage and tender Him service, our memory, understanding and will, begging Him to possess them and rule them and work through them, so that their action may be not so much theirs as His.

We may ask Him to claim for Himself more place in our *memory*, a more frequent and loving remembrance of Him as the hours of the day go by, that we may fall back naturally so to say on the thought of Him in the intervals of our various duties, to renew our morning intention of doing all and suffering all for His sake, to find contentment in Him however things fall out, and to increase our love by the aspirations which, easily and swiftly made, yet bear eternal fruit.

We may offer Him our *understanding*, to be more enlightened on this or that mystery of the Faith, on our duties and responsibilities, on the difference between the things of time and those of eternity.

And, chief of all, we may offer Him our *will* on the regulation of which all our relations with Him depend. If we have feelings of devotion we may well be thankful for they help very much. If we have none, we must not be disquieted for they are not necessary. The will is what God looks to, and this is always in our power. But it is weak and wayward, and shies at every difficulty. Our Lord comes mainly on its account, to give it strength of purpose, vigour in action, constancy under trial, wisdom in choice, generosity in sacrifice, perseverance in monotonous duty, endurance to the end.

But *we must ask* for all this. Have we ever noticed how much more readily we ask for light than for strength? Perhaps because we imagine the first will involve no great suffering, or is further removed from it, whilst strength is asked in view of a cross directly facing us, or of an effort to be called for presently. We act as if God were more liberal of light than of strength. When we know His Will, instead of thanking Him and going on to ask for courage to carry it out, we sit down and cry because we feel so weak. Yet God only gives the first grace for the sake of the second. He never means to leave us halfway through a trouble, but He does mean us to ask for the help we need. And after Communion is the time for asking: "This is your hour," He says to us then, "Ask, and you shall receive."

Besides the powers of our souls, we may bring to Him our desires. How they run riot! Over a thousand fields they wander, without reference to the journey's end, without any nobler purpose than self-gratification, wasting on baubles the energy and affection of our immortal souls. It is hard to control them, but our Lord will take them in hand when He comes. He will teach us to hold them firmly within their proper bounds—the Holy Will of God, that shelter in which we should rest like a bird in its nest. All It contains is good for us; everything outside, however attractive, is not only beyond our needs but would prove harmful to us.

We may bring to Him our anxieties and our hopes, our resolutions, our failures of the day before, perhaps a victory here and there, a perplexing question to be solved, a difficult letter to be written—what, indeed may we not bring! It is our Friend who is with us, keenly interested in all we tell Him, glad as in the days of His life on earth to be led about wherever He is needed, wherever His healing hand and Omnipotent word and tender pitying glance may do their work. He is the same now as when He was to be found among the sick and poor and in the house of mourning, with the same yearning to help us every one—but *we must ask, we must ask.* We receive not, because we ask not, or because, says St. James, we "ask amiss",[1] that is, without the necessary dispositions, or for things that would not profit us. "If any of you want wisdom," he says, "let him ask of God who giveth to all abundantly and upbraideth not, and it shall be given him."[2] He takes for granted that our prayer will not be for the necessaries of this life alone, but for the "better gifts" for which St. Paul would have us zealous[3] "the things by which we truly live."[4]

What childish requests some of ours will seem when seen in the light of eternity! what poor paltry gifts to have taken up all our thoughts when we were in the audience chamber of the King of kings, or rather, when He was giving audience in our chamber, enjoying our hospitality, and therefore under an obligation to show Himself royally bountiful. "Why," we shall say—if not in Heaven at least in Purgatory, the land of vain regrets—"oh why did we not profit better by that time of grace, to secure the enduring treasures that might have been had

---

1   James 4:3.   2   James 1:5.   3   1 Cor. 12:31.
4   Mass for 6th Sunday after Epiphany.

for the asking—strength in temptation, light to see our way, Wisdom, Counsel, Fortitude, Holy Fear—Gifts, that would have made all the difference to our life on earth and to our eternal life in Heaven!"

Giveth to all abundantly—to all, therefore to me, and abundantly, especially at this "acceptable time" when having given Himself He will surely give us all things.

Upbraiding not—welcome reassuring words. The poor who present themselves confidently the first or second time at the rich man's gate, fear to be thought importunate and to meet rebuff when they come again and again the winter through. The friend who has been shabby with his friend hesitates to ask a kindness next time he is in need, and if he ventures, fears the word of well deserved expostulation or reproach. So it is with us—but not with God. We have no reproach to fear when, having thrown away His grace, we ask for more; when, having shown ourselves stingy or cowardly, self-seeking in any of our wonted ways, we come to Him for comfort and for help.

Petition to such a One ought to be an easy task. Yet, unless we are on our guard we may often omit it in our Acts of thanksgiving after Communion, and let the King take back with Him the gifts He meant to leave.

"What wilt thou that I do for thee?" He asks with Divine kindness each time He comes—*we must have our answer ready.*

XXXV

"DOMINE NON SUM DIGNUS!"

PERHAPS the prevalent feeling of most of us about our Communions, is distress at the callousness which nothing can rouse or remove—neither the marvels there wrought for us, nor the love there testified us, nor the abundance of treasure there laid up for us.

On the other hand, some of us are possessed by so strong a sense of our unworthiness, that it keeps us from the Communion rails altogether. Instead of saying "Come Lord Jesus," with St. John, they cry out with St. Peter: "Depart from me, O Lord, for I am a sinner."

Peter knew his Master well enough to dare to make such a prayer. A humble, trustful acknowledgement of his unworthiness was the last thing in the world likely to drive Christ from him. His lips said "Depart," whilst his heart held fast Him whom he loved, for whom he had left all things. If our "Depart from me, O Lord," or our "Domine non sum dignus," is said in this spirit of trustful love, it will not keep us away from Christ but drive us to Him. True humility draws near and holds out its hand for the help it needs. It is discouragement, the devil's counterfeit of humility—and a very bad one— that keeps aloof.

The devil is a cleverer logician than we are, but a good way of worsting him in argument is to admit his premises and deny his conclusion. "Lord, I am not worthy, therefore I will stay away," would be his suggestion. It sounds plausible enough, but being an enemy's, it is at least open to suspicion, and it is in direct opposition to the teaching of the Church and of Scripture: "Since we have no merit to plead, assist us by Thy protection."[1] "What shall I do, whither shall I fly but to Thee, my God, *for* I have sinned exceedingly in my life."[2] If we have sinned, if we are unworthy, what refuge have we but Him; who else can forgive, and reassure, and comfort and strengthen us? "Lord, to whom shall we go?" we must all say to Him with Peter. And His answer will be: "Come to Me all…all you who are heavy burdened come, and I will refresh you."

True humility drives us *to* Christ, not away from Him. To think and act otherwise, and be so fixed in our view that neither God nor man can move us, would be a species of humility to be found neither in Heaven nor on earth, one that neither God nor man would recognise.

How different from this is the simplicity which here, as in all things else, follows the lead of the Church, listens to the Voice of the Chief Shepherd and goes where he leads; which, conscious on the one hand of its weakness and need, and on the other, of the dignity of the Sacrament, thanks God for the distinct expression of His Will in these later times, for the clear statement of the few dispositions which

1   Secret, Second Sunday of Advent.   2   Office for the Dead.

ensure a good Communion, and thus reassured, goes in humble trust, goes often to the Holy Table, not because it is worthy, but because it is needy and poor.

The controversies of the past are silenced, and when the Vicar of Christ has spoken so decisively, will not those who still hang back deserve the reproach: "Why do you halt between two ways? if the Lord be God, follow Him."[1] If you believe that the Vicar of Christ speaks to you with His authority and declares to you His good pleasure, trust him rather than the vagaries of your own mind, to which no such assistance is promised, and follow him with docility and trust when he beckons you to the altar of God.

---

1   3 Kings 18:21.

XXXVI

"REASONABLE SERVICE"

(Rom. 12:1.)

NOT ONLY as we read the lives of the Saints, but also in the guidance of our own lives, it behooves us to bear in mind that the Author of Nature and Grace is one and the same, that the dictates of Reason and Grace can never be really at variance, and that however much Grace may supersede Reason, it can never contradict it.

Reason will certainly not take us all the way we have to go, nor suffice for every need, but it can never be left behind. We must take stock of our mental, physical, and spiritual outfit and not overtax them under pretext of mortification or zeal. "Reasonable service," he tells us who "laboured more than all the Apostles," is what God asks of us.

Views will differ considerably as to what is reasonable, and those with a clear tendency to self-sparing are hardly safe judges in this matter. Under the guidance of grace Saints do things that it would be rash for us to attempt. But this is only saying that what is reasonable in them would not be so in ourselves. Their spiritual equipment is on a grander scale, their correspondence with grace of a higher order; the habits they have laboriously formed render them capable of heroic efforts, eminently reasonable in them; but for us to attempt the same would be presumption and end in disaster. Till we have made their preparation, we must follow on their track at a distance; learn to deny ourselves in the discharge of ordinary duty; listen with greater docility to the invitations of grace, and undertake honestly and steadily the contest with self to which with quiet persistence it urges us. Not to admit this; or, on the other hand, to expect to follow Christ without pain and to purchase the Kingdom of Heaven without cost, would be manifestly unreasonable. The road thither must be uphill, therefore wearisome, the struggle with self can never be anything but a disagreeable process—all this stands to reason.

It is not those who question these truths or who minimise them in practise, who have need to bear in mind the counsel of the Apostle. But those whose ear is ever open to the whisperings of grace, who are training themselves to make sacrifices readily, whose main desire is to know the Will of God and do It at any cost—such as these must be guided by the wise counsel of St. Paul if they would not be drawn aside into unsafe paths, urged, but not by the Spirit of God, into what is above their strength, with the probable result of a reaction sooner or later, of falling into discouragement, and of throwing up everything in despair.

A German picture of the Guardian Angel shows his little pilgrim charge walking warily, staff and beads in hand, along a narrow winding path, from which a precipice falls sheer down on either side. The heavenly Guardian follows close behind, the protecting hands ready to check the least swerve to right or left, for a tempting fringe of flowering roses hides the edge of the road, and deadly peril awaits the unguarded step.

So is it with us all. There is danger in excess no less than in defect. What involves strain will not last. We must govern ourselves wisely, follow grace, not precede it, be aware of our limitations, deal with ourselves at times as we should deal with others when health is plainly demanding more than ordinary consideration. We are composed of soul—and body. One danger of forgetting this and of bringing the body to bay, is that it is apt to act unmistakably on the defensive and end by remaining master of the field.

St. Ignatius, speaking from his own experience, tells us that when the Spirit of God is laying siege to a soul, He troubles and disconcerts it, but when He is in possession, His action is to pacify and reassure and lead it on its way in peace.

The practice of the evil one, on the contrary, is to lull to sleep the slothful and self-indulgent soul and those he already holds fast bound in the chains of sin. But a soul that has escaped him, and every soul following Christ seriously, he is wont, at one time or another, to pursue with vain fears, troubled desires, promptings to impracticable, or useless, or hurtful excesses, so to lead it astray, or tire it out on a path too difficult for it to keep.

This insight into the workings of the Spirit of God and of the evil spirit, is of incalculable value to us in our daily life. We come continually under one or other of these influences, we are perpetually called upon to make choices, and it is all important for us to be able to determine the character of the agency by which we are swayed.

"But," some will say, "to know the source of the impulse that moves me, I must know the state of my own soul, and this is of all things in the world what I am most ignorant about."

Is it? Are you absolutely ignorant as to whether you are living in grievous and habitual and unscrupulous violation of the law of God or in the fixed resolution to refuse Him something He is asking with a clearness and persistency in which you cannot but recognise His voice? Or are you, on the other hand—not absolutely certain as to the condition of your state before God, for "no man knows" with full certitude "whether he is worthy of love or of hatred"[1]—but conscious through the honest inward testimony which you would feel justified in accepting as sufficient in the case of another, that you desire to love and serve God, and are not aware of any resistance to His known Will in any important matter?

Surely in a normal state of soul, when the light of reason is not obscured by scrupulosity, we are able to give such an answer to these questions as an enlightened friend who knows us well would recognise as the truth? If a man knows clearly when with full knowledge, advertence, and consent he has yielded to grievous sin, may he not know— again supposing a normal state of soul when he is capable of forming a judgement—that he has not so sinned?

---

1 Ecclus. 9:1.

It should not, then, in that frank intercourse with God which makes Him welcome to the secrets of the heart and conscience, be impossible to conclude with moral certainty that we are His friends, weak, maybe, and very faulty, yet sincere; to believe that He treats us as His friends, and, therefore, that thoughts and impulses which leave us troubled and discouraged are not from Him and consequently are not to be heeded.

"Peace I leave with you, My peace I give unto you,"[1] are our dear Master's words. He does not overtax; His yoke is not too heavy. There are indeed seasons when He calls for the soul's whole energy and generosity to respond to His call. But always, whether in these crises, the momentous epochs of life, or along our daily path, with the help of ordinary grace that beckons to quiet fidelity and easy sacrifice, we are to pursue our way in peace and trust. Effort and struggle, even when exceptionally strenuous and painful, are not incompatible with the peace and prudence which mark the workings of the spirit of God, and with the teaching of the great Apostle who, in his Master's interests, called upon the first fervent followers of their Lord for "reasonable service."

---

1   John 14:27.

XXXVII

TRUE LOVE

"I also have a heart like you." (Job 12:3.)

THE DISCIPLE. "And therefore, O Lord, Thou canst sympathise with me in every pain of body and mind, in the trouble that is upon me now. I too am heavy and sad. I too can say: 'My soul is sorrowful.' Pain and anxiety are stifling it, the weight of the cross bears me down, my burden seems more than I can bear. I see no quarter whence help can come, and though I try to trust and resign myself to Thy Will, I cannot throw off the trouble or dismiss the fears. And so I come to Thee for the sympathy and refreshment Thou hast promised to the heavy-laden."

Christ. "And you do well, child. You have the fellow-feeling of My Heart to an extent you could neither ask nor dream of. But I would have you find strength and comfort where I found it. I would have you remember that if I am your Friend on whom you may rightly count for sympathy, you are also Mine of whom I may expect a little generosity. Is it the part of generosity to make much of cost and sacrifice in the service of a friend, to protest vehemently whilst accepting labour and pain for His sake? Or is it our wont rather to hide our suffering from him, to smile lest he should see and be saddened by our tears, to seek to convince him by loving words that the joy of sharing trial with him or doing him a service far outweighs any little cost to ourselves? See if My Heart has not shown this instinct of true friendship in Its dealings with you, and if your heart cannot brace itself to make Me a return in kind.

You are My disciple and follower. When I ask you to show yourself such not in word and in tongue but in deed and in truth; when, going before you carrying My Cross, I turn round to see if you are near to give Me comfort by your companionship; when I prove My love by counting on yours for proofs of faithful and generous friendship—do not fail Me then.

And, child, believe Me, this is the easiest way to suffer as well as the most meritorious. Try, and you will find it so. You will not have less of My sympathy and My help because you forget yourself for Me, and think more of the joy there is in following Me nearly than of the pain. It was the thought of you that solaced Me through the hardships of the three and thirty years and the dark hours of the Passion. Try what love of Me, a generous self-forgetting love, will do to lighten the cross that weighs upon you now. I am waiting for an effort, for a smile. Can you not give them to Me? Try."

> "In what place soever Thou shall be, Lord my King,
> there will Thy servant be." (2 Kings 15:21.)

The Disciple. Dear Lord, I bring Thee my cross and lay it down at Thy feet as a love offering. With Thy help I will take it up again and bear it patiently, bravely, perseveringly. But I want more than this. I want my offering to be a return in kind, a token of grateful love to Thee for that love of me which filled Thy Heart when Thou didst bear Thy heavy cross to Calvary. I want to be Thy companion on that road, to comfort Thee by sharing Thy pain of body and of mind. Thou art my Chief, I will follow wherever Thou dost lead. In what place soever Thou shalt be, O Lord my King, there will Thy servant be. Thou art my Bridegroom, my place is at Thy side. Thou art my Friend, to be treated as one dearly loved.

I will not then make much of what I do or bear for Thy sake. I will not be forever obtruding upon Thy notice my weariness or my repugnance. Rather will I seek to hide the shrinking of nature. I will take as a matter of course the cost of following such a Leader, and think more of the honour and the joy than of the pain. I will count Thy contentment in my companionship abundant compensation for any labour and any suffering.

Look round, dear Lord, as Thou goest before me on the uphill road, look round and see me close behind, getting as near to Thee as I can, stumbling, falling again and again, but up at once and pressing closer than before, never faltering in my purpose to give Thee a loyal, true, generous service, as free from self-seeking as Thy example and Thy grace will enable it to be.

"Help me, O Lord, in this my resolution, and give me grace now this day perfectly to begin for all I have hitherto done is nothing."[1]

---

1 *Imit.*, Book 1, ch. 19.

XXXVIII

"BE READY"

"Be you then also ready, for at what hour you think not, the Son of Man will come." (Luke 12:40.)

WHAT is it to be ready?

First and essentially, it is to be in a state of grace, for should Death surprise us in mortal sin we are lost for ever. But shall we count this bare requisite enough? In His prayer to His Eternal Father on the eve of His Passion our Lord said: "I have finished the work Thou gavest Me to do." And lying on His hard deathbed, it was only after the words: "It is finished," that "bowing His Head He gave up the ghost."

Were He to come to me now in death, would He find me able to say: "I have finished the work Thou gavest me to do, for my own soul and for those whom Thou hast entrusted to me and of whom I must give an account"? Could I say at least that I am labouring earnestly at this now?

When we stand on the wharf, bound for a distant country, we cast a look around us to see if all things are ready. We look at the well-filled boxes and trunks, and wonder if we have forgotten anything that should be there.

In case the requisites of life, as we consider them, are not to be had in the land to which we are going, we shall have taken care to provide them beforehand. What an amount of foresight and prudence does that luggage represent! Nothing has been left to chance, every need has been thought out and provided for in time.

I am standing now on that stage to which my summons may come at any moment. Am I ready for the distant Land for which I am bound and which is to be my eternal dwelling-place? Once my vessel has pushed off, the time for preparation will be past—Am I ready?

I look around—the forgiveness of my sins, has it been secured? my good works, are they there ready? my talents, have they been multiplied and used to His glory who gave them? "Thou oughtest to have committed my money to the bankers and at my coming I should have received my own with usury."[1] I mark the words "my money... my own." All belongs to God, all is given for a purpose, or rather lent; my gifts, my time, my money, my influence, my very life, are but a loan. I shall have to render a strict account "when my life which is lent me shall be called for again."[2]

"Trade till I come,"[3] is His charge to all. Is my trading such as to earn the "*Euge, serve bone!*—Well done, good and faithful servant!" when I come before Him to give an account of my stewardship? I notice that it does not suffice to have done no harm with the talents confided to us, we must have put them out to our Master's profit. I notice again that no excuse is accepted. I shall not be able to plead circumstances, or the insignificance of the trust committed

---

1 Matth. 25:27.   2 Wisd. 15:8.   3 Luke 19:13.

to me if I appear before Him with empty hands: "Had I been differently situated, had I been given the talents of So-and-so I might have done something with my life." We know the awful answer the unprofitable servant received. It is not the result but the loyal service to which God looks. Everyone is of use. Everyone's work of head and hand and heart is wanted. Each has a mission of his own, a labour in his own sphere and surroundings that God waits to reward. We are each and all bound to look around us and see what work has been laid at our door, assigned us from eternity as the material for our everlasting crown.

In one sense God needs none of us, in another He needs us everyone. He can spare no one. He wants my service and will condescend to receive from my hand what He will accept from no other. What a stimulus to joyous activity is here! I must accustom myself to look not at the nature of the work that falls to my lot but at the Hand from which it comes and in which I place it; at the Eye that notes it; at the Heart that treasures it. This will deprive toil of its monotony and make it precious in my sight as it is in His.

And what about my time, the most precious of the talents confided to me? Does my Master look with approval at the mapping out of my day, at the portion set aside for prayer, for serious work, for the duties of my state; and at the due proportion—as I consider it—devoted to relaxation and amusement? How shall I look back on my employment of days and weeks and years when the Angel of Death shall come to me with the announcement "that time shall be no more"[1] for me, that the harvest I have sown

---

1   Apoc. 10:6.

"And there appeared to them parted tongues as it were of fire, and it sat upon every one of them: And they were all filled with the Holy Ghost." (Acts 2:3-4.)

is ripe and the hour has come to reap?[1]

Other things, too, are to be made ready against that hour. What about the virtues that make up the apparel "glittering and white"[2] in which my soul must be arrayed to take its place in those pure ranks into which there shall not enter anything defiled?[3] Do I often and carefully wash my robes and make them white in the blood of the Lamb[4] by sacramental confession and frequent acts of contrition?

Am I providing a store of charity against my day of need, the charity that covers a multitude of sins? Do I set a watch upon my lips and deeds and thoughts lest my neighbour suffer hurt through me? "Come, blessed of My Father," the King will say at the Judgement, "for I was hungry and you gave Me to eat; I was thirsty and you gave Me to drink; I was a stranger and you took me in; naked and you covered Me; sick and you visited Me; I was in prison and you came to Me...Amen I say to you, as long as you did it to one of My least brethren you did it to Me."[5] How many of these works of charity to His suffering members, that is to Himself, am I preparing for His acceptance and reward?

Thus, then, as I stand waiting for my summons, may I profitably pass in review the needs of a future day, and like a wise traveller—provide in time.

---

1   Apoc. 14:15.   2   Apoc. 19:8.   3   Apoc. 21:27.
4   Apoc. 7:14.   5   Matth. 25:40.

XXXIX

VISITS

*"All the day I have spread forth My hands to
an unbelieving people."* (Isaias 65:2.)

HIS was bad enough, but to appeal in vain all day
and every day to a believing people, is infinitely
worse. Our Lord tells us that every good tree
brings forth good fruit[1] and St. James says: "faith without
works is dead."[2] Would an impartial observer of our life
and habits conclude we have a strong, practical faith in the
Real Presence? We would die, please God, in defence of it,
should the need come. But do we live by it and for it? Do
we in this one matter of Visits show the efficacious faith
that might be expected of us?

If a person of note comes to live in our neighbourhood
we call to pay our respects; if he is a friend we are eager to
bid him welcome, are delighted to have him near at hand
to consult and help and bring home with us and make
much of; to sympathise with if he is in trouble, to make his
interests one with our own.

Is there anything of this in our relations with our
Lord, who lives, maybe, not too far from us to expect the

---

1   Matth. 7:17.   2   James 2:20.

ordinary courtesy we show to neighbours? Do we go to Him to pay Him the homage due to His Majesty, to thank Him for all He does for us and is ready to do for us there, to show Him sympathy for the neglect and irreverence to which He exposes Himself for our sakes, and to make Him welcome to any little service His condescension may ask of us, to confide to Him our secrets and anxieties, delight Him with some unexpected piece of generosity, ask for ourselves and others the favours He is longing to bestow? Or has He to say to His Father, as part of His perpetual sacrifice for us: "Friend and neighbour Thou hast put far from Me"[1]?

To ascertain the worth of a thing there is nothing like comparison. Let us see how our dispositions compare with the Psalmist's in this point of visiting the house of the Lord.

Possibly the unvarnished truth about ourselves might be something like this:

"I believe, O Lord, that Thou art really present, Body and Blood, Soul and Divinity upon this altar, a few steps from my home; but because I do not see Thee there my faith in Thy Presence does not attract me to Thee:

I believe Thou dost invite to Thee the labourers and the heavy-burdened; but because I do not hear Thy Voice and Thy invitation, I do not feel moved to go to Thee for Thy promised refreshment:

I believe that my every word would be heard, every trouble compassionated, every perplexity enlightened, every anxiety shared, every trial sanctified; but because I should not have the consolation of any sensible response to my confidences, I have no heart to take my troubles to Thy feet:

---

1   Ps. 87:19.

I am deeply conscious that I need help and guidance; but unless I can have them in the way I want, I do not care to seek them:

I am truly sensible of Thy goodness in remaining always in our midst to receive our homage and be our resource in every need; but as I find no special pleasure in paying my court to Thee, and can trace no particular favour to such service of Thee, I cannot bring myself to do more than is of strict obligation:

I never visit Thee, not because my days are too full, but because my heart is too empty of the love that would make this mark of affection a delight to me. It would cost me too much. I should not know what to say. I should feel constrained in Thy presence, and therefore, O Lord—I never come."

So much for *our* desire for the Courts of the Lord. Now let us hear the Psalmist's raptures at the thought of the Temple which with all its glory was so poor a type of the reality to come:

"As the hart panteth after the fountains of water, so panteth my soul after Thee, O God!" for "the place of the wonderful tabernacle, even the house of God."[1]

"How lovely are Thy tabernacles, O Lord of Hosts, my soul longeth and fainteth for the courts of the Lord....Thy altars, O Lord of Hosts, my King and my God! For better is one day in Thy courts above thousands."[2]

"I rejoiced at what was said to me: We shall go into the house of the Lord."[3]

"Come, let us praise the Lord with joy...let us come before His Presence with thanksgiving."[4]

---

1   Ps. 41:5.   2   Ps. 83:11.   3   Ps. 121:1.
4   Ps. 94:2.

"Come in before His Presence with exceeding great joy."[1]

"Come and see the works of God…come and hear and I will tell you what great things He hath done for my soul."[2]

"Bless the Lord, O my soul, and never forget all He hath done for thee."[3]

"We will praise Thee, O God, we will praise."[4]

What would the Psalmist have done had our chances been his! Would his full heart have found excuses to keep him from the Altar and the Tabernacle? Would he have felt his need of worship less because his God was so hidden and so humble? Because, instead of the Temple's glorious courts, He had contented Himself with the meanest of lodgings? Would he have found his ardour abated because in place of figures he had the reality? Would he have been absent from the House of the Lord because no sensible consolation was vouchsafed him, or have expected to see in order to adore and praise?

Sweet Singer of Israel, if figures and prophecy and hope so inspired thee that we turn to thy glowing fervour to warm our own cold hearts, what would it have been hadst thou possessed the sacramental God, Jesus in the Eucharist, to content thy longing and prompt thy gratitude and thy love!

What kings and prophets have desired to see, I see and may see daily if I will. Here I may come to adore and praise my God, to propitiate my Judge, to thank my constant Benefactor, to converse with my best Friend, to get counsel in doubt, strength and comfort in trouble, more grace, more light, more generosity—help in every need.

---

1   Ps. 99:2.   2   Ps. 65:5.   3   Ps. 102:2.
4   Ps. 74:2.

It will not be so long: "You have not Me always," our Lord tells us. When life is done, and from the threshold of eternity we look back on the days of the Altar and the Tabernacle, what sorrow it will be to us that while time and opportunity were ours, we let—not necessary duties, but the weakness of faith and love—keep us from Him who all life through waited patiently for us there and with tender pleading tried to draw us to Himself!

My God, I will come to Thee. This must not go on. Death must not find me like this. I could not bear at Judgement to hear Thee say sadly: "So long have I been with you and have you not known Me!"[1] I will come to Thee; just because of my miserable dispositions, I will come. Because I am cold I will come to the fire and humbly beg a little warmth. Because I am self-seeking, I will come and learn the forgetfulness of self which none can teach like Thee. Because I am poor and needy in every way, I will draw near to Thee who canst enrich me. Because it will please Thee to see me at Thy feet, I will come. What if for awhile I find no change in myself! What if the pleasure of the visit is all on Thy side! I can be a little generous—at last. To serve Thee at my own cost will enhance, perhaps, not lessen, the value of my gift in Thy eyes? Teach me how to speak to Thee, to bring my joys and sorrows, my plans and difficulties and aspirations after better things to Thee, and come at length to run to Thee in every need as to my Friend.

---

1   John 14:9.

X L

WILLFULNESS

I F ONLY we could be penetrated here on earth with the reverence which is the very atmosphere of Heaven! Before "the Most High God," the Seraphim cover their faces with their wings[1] and sing continually: "Holy, Holy, Holy." "Thousands of thousands minister to Him, and ten thousand times a hundred thousand stand before Him."[2] And Saints fall down on their faces and adore Him and "cast their crowns before the Throne."[3]

Meantime men on earth are discovering discrepancies in His revelation, deriding the possibility of miracles, criticising the government of the world, denying any government of it that supposes a Governor, and doing their best to explain away all evidence of the supernatural.

Many who do not go to this length habitually ignore the Commandments of God. They call Him to account when His plans conflict with their own. They look upon His gifts—fortune, health, honour, influence, the possession of those dear to them—as their right, and when He reclaims

---

1   Isaias 6:2.   2   Dan. 7:10.   3   Apoc. 4:10.

any of these, either complain bitterly as of an injustice, or cut themselves off from intercourse with Him as they would with an offending neighbour. They will not consider His rights or His designs of mercy in their afflictions. They reject His offers of strength and consolation, entrench themselves in a sullen reserve, and drift into a state of estrangement from Him which lasts, maybe, till death. There may have been times when something like this was true of ourselves.

And God is patient with us in our perversity, whilst the Angels see with amazement our forgetfulness of what is due to His Majesty. How far man can forget himself in treating with God, and abuse the Divine condescension by insolence and churlishness, we may learn from what the prophet Isaias tells us of Achaz, king of Juda, when his powerful neighbour, the king of Syria, was coming against him:

"And the Lord said to Isaias: Go forth to meet Achaz and say to him: Fear not and let not thy heart be afraid.... Thus saith the Lord God: This shall not be....And the Lord spoke again to Achaz saying: Ask thee a sign of the Lord thy God unto the depth of hell or unto the height above.

And Achaz said: I will not ask, and I will not tempt the Lord."[1]

Such perversity astounds us. Yet something very like this we do ourselves when we meet God's advances with surly refusals; as if it were a manly act to show ourselves thankless and boorish towards the Lord of Heaven and earth!

---

1   Isaias 7:12.

Do we suppose our refractoriness will defeat His designs? Surely not. He needs none of us. It is only by an act of supreme condescension that He stoops to ask our service. If we refuse it, the loss is wholly ours. Others will profit by our foolishness and show themselves more worthy of His favour. So it has been from the beginning: "I will not serve"[1], said Lucifer, and like lightning he fell from Heaven. God's glory was unimpaired. Preeminence among the angelic host was but transferred; Michael became its leader and "prince of all the souls to be received." Of one of the Twelve it was said: "his bishopric let another take,"[2] and the office even of an Apostle passed from Judas to Matthias.

"Be not deceived, God is not mocked," says St. Paul, "for what things a man shall sow, those also shall he reap."[3] The Divine patience with us is inexplicable. God offers His gifts—nay, presses them upon our acceptance. But He will not force our free-will. One of the most solemn lessons taught on Calvary was this.

Save Thyself and us! The central cross drew to itself the imploring eyes of the thieves on either side. He who hung between them felt with the sympathy of experience the anguish of His fellow sufferers and yearned most truly to save them both. Grace was not wanting; the Blood to purchase salvation for both was being profusely shed. Truly there was plentiful redemption at hand—and for both. How came it, then, that one alone profited by it when the chances seemed so equal? Both were malefactors, both, apparently, began by blaspheming, both had before their

1   Jerem. 2:20.   2   Acts 1:20.   3   Gal. 6:8.

eyes the same Divine example of meekness and patience. The miraculous darkness, the earthquake, the prodigies on earth and in the heavens that made the multitude go home striking their breasts, and the Centurian exclaim: "Indeed this man was the Son of God!"—all these actual graces were for both.

The difference between them lay in the willingness of the one and the willfulness of the other when there was a question of accepting, not the salvation for which they cried, but that offered them by God. One let grace have its way with him. He saw that Form beside him sink lower and lower on the nails. He marked the silence of those uncomplaining lips. He heard the prayer: "Father, forgive them," the only answer torture and the reviling crowd could wring from that meek Heart. And as he looked and listened, there came upon him a strong impulse to put from him the wild desire for release and life for which his companion was clamouring, and crave instead, of Him who hung there, a remembrance of mercy. He surrendered himself to the impulse. He laid hold of the proffered salvation, and turning to Jesus cried: "Lord, remember me when Thou shalt come into Thy kingdom." The act by which he yielded himself up to the Will of God, and flung himself on the mercy of his Redeemer, and humbly accepted his punishment in satisfaction for his sins—it was this that saved him.

The other thief saw the same Divine example, heard the same Divine words. But the way of grace into his soul was barred by the frantic desire of release from his torments, which consumed him. No other salvation would he accept.

He might have followed his companion's lead, and his prayer for a remembrance would have met with the same merciful response. But he hardened his heart; he let the hour of mercy pass and the whispers of grace die down in his soul, and despair came to fill up his cup of misery.

God will not save us in spite of ourselves; we must acknowledge His overlordship, submit ourselves to Him, and take His Will in place of our own if we are to find rest to our souls. We cannot be petulant with Him, dictate conditions to Him, or let His marvellous condescension to us make us forget who we are. No intimacy, no privilege can authorise anyone to take liberties with Him. St. Thomas nearly lost his faith and his apostleship, and all the fruit of his courageous love of his Master, by the willfulness which made him presume to prescribe the conditions for his belief.

The higher the Saints mount in the knowledge and love of God, the more absolute is the reverence and submission by which they liken themselves to the blessed inhabitants of Heaven and earn their place among them. The loftiest of all there, the Mother of God and Queen of Angels and Saints, is His handmaid always. Nay, Christ Himself, as Man our "Advocate with the Father"[1] is heard still—"for His reverence."[2]

The temper of the modern mind is self-assertion and independence. Reverence and submission are at a discount in the world of today. But in Heaven they retain their value always: if we want to reach our place there, we must be shaping for it now.

---

1   1 John 2:1.   2   Heb. 5:7.

XLI

THIRST

ONE of the characteristics of the Messiah foretold by the Prophets was His self-effacement. "He shall not cry, neither shall His voice be heard in the streets."[1] He was to be at once "glorious, and secret, and hidden,"[2] "poor and in labours from His youth,"[3] "the teacher of little ones,"[4] "verily a hidden God."[5]

The fullness of time came, and "the prophets were found faithful."[6] "When all things were in quiet silence and night was in the midst of her course,"[7] the Word was made flesh and dwelt amongst us. For thirty years He lived unknown in an obscure village; and when the time came for Him to manifest Himself to men, when His days were ablaze with the splendour of the miracles needed to accredit His mission, when "the whole world had gone after Him,"[8] even then the atmosphere of humility that shrouded all this, kept Him the hidden God.

His ways were quiet, His teaching was quiet. So that when we hear that on a certain day, "the last and great

---

1 Isaias 42:2.   2 Ecclus. 11:4.   3 Ps. 87:16.
4 Isaias 33:18.   5 Isaias 45:15.   6 Ecclus. 36:18.
7 Wisd. 18:14.   8 John 12:19.

day of the Feast (of Tabernacles) Jesus stood and cried, saying: If any man thirst, let him come to Me and drink,"[1] we are at once startled to attention by the departure from His ordinary self-repression. It must, we feel, have some special significance and call for reverent study.

With a multitude about Him, He stood and cried: "If any man thirst let him come to Me and drink." What was the purport of the cry that betrayed the fullness of His Heart that day? It was an appeal to each and every one of those whose human nature He shares, for this thirst is upon us all—the child at school, the philosopher, the merchant, the poet, the scoundrel, the saint, are stirred every one of them by the God-given craving for happiness which is the end of our creation. Every joy and sorrow of human life has its source in it; every pursuit points to it; Art in all her highest aspirations is the expression of it; Religion directs it steadily to the living fountains where alone it can be satisfied.

This thirst for happiness is at once our need and our glory, so much a necessity of our nature that no abuse can stifle it, so true a witness to the nobility of that nature and to the grandeur of our destiny, that men are forced to own nothing here can quench it. God Who made us for Himself has put into our hearts a thirst for Him that it may lead us to the happiness to which it points. We may not recognise it as tending to Him, we may think to assuage it by one or other of the baits that life holds out to us—wealth, pleasure, glory, love—but sooner or later we come to learn by experience that, instead of slaking, these things do but increase our thirst. Solomon who had

1 John 7:37.

enjoyed them all tells us: "I have given my heart to know prudence, and learning, and errors, and folly. I said: I will go and abound in delights and enjoy good things....I built me houses and planted vineyards,...I made gardens and orchards, I got me men-servants and maidservants and had a great family....I heaped together for myself silver and gold and the wealth of kings...and whatsoever my eyes desired I refused them not: and I withheld not my heart from enjoying every pleasure. And when I turned myself to all the works my hands had wrought, and to the labours wherein I had laboured in vain, I saw in all things vanity and vexation of mind...and therefore was I weary of my life, and I hated all my application wherewith I had earnestly laboured."[1] St. Augustine went on the same quest and came to the same conclusion: "Thou hast made us for Thyself, O Lord, and our hearts are restless until they rest in Thee."

Yet the bulk of men profit nothing by a universal experience. It may be the lot of all, but he himself—each one believes or hopes—will prove an exception, and so, having fixed their goal they pursue it with a patience and perseverance that makes the heart bleed to think of the disillusioning and disappointment to which they are doomed.

> "Water, water everywhere
> And not a drop to drink."

"Salt water cannot yield sweet"[2], and the things of this life, however fair their promise, defeat our expectation when we make them an end. It is not their fault but ours,

---

1   Ecclesiastes 2   2   James 3:12.

who would force them to serve a purpose for which they were never made.

The child St. Augustine watched by the seashore tried in vain to fill with water the hole his little hands had scooped. Again and again he fetched water from the sea, but as fast as he poured it in, the thirsty sand drank it up and waited for more. And we shall never satisfy with anything of this world the hearts made to enjoy the Infinite God.

But we try, most of us—try all our lives. Meantime One is standing by, watching and pitying: "My people have done two evils, they have forsaken Me, the fountain of living water, and have digged to themselves cisterns, broken cisterns, that can hold no water."[1]

The same pity stirred the Heart of Christ the day He stood and cried: "If any man thirst, let him come to Me and drink." There is something very solemn and moving in this cry of the Incarnate Son of God. It is the complaint of old, renewed by human lips, renewed a second time, for He had said before this: "You will not come to Me that you may have life."[2] He is one of us; He knows how much we need Him; He feels for us with a human sympathy, and in our perversity it is the harm we do ourselves rather than the injury to Himself that He seems to deplore.

If any man thirst. "If thou didst know the gift of God thou wouldst perhaps have asked of Him and He would have given thee living water."[3] So courteously He puts His invitation, and solicits our free will. He knows how we all thirst, but He must bide our time. "He shall not be

1   Jerem. 2:13.   2   John 5:40.   3   John 4:10.

troublesome," His prophet had said of Him[1] and He seems to fear lest in His desire to help us He might be deemed over importunate and insistent.

Not once alone, nor to a Jewish multitude only, did the Heart of Christ send forth that cry to thirsting souls: "All the day I have spread forth My hands to an unbelieving people who walk in a way that is not good."[2] His call is to every soul that comes into this world, and if ever there was need to pause in the rush of life to give ear to Him, it is in these days of ours. "Come to Me," He says, "and drink. On every side you will find the allurements of sense multiplying continually in number and fascination. But they will never satisfy you—Come to Me!"

All that goes to make up worldliness—the contentment with things present, the ignoring of God and the supernatural, impatience with the restraints of faith and religion, pride of intellect, the glorification of man in the triumphant subjection of Nature's hidden and marvellous forces, the worship of material wellbeing, the wringing out of creatures whatever may minister to ease and pleasure— all this will increase as time goes on and the end nears. And the result will be to deaden in men the craving for the things that constitute true life.

We see, then, why the Lover of our souls is so urgent, why He stands and cries to each one of us during our short day of life here: "Come to Me!" As Man He knows experimentally, in a way He did not know before the Incarnation, the thirst of the human soul for its God: "I thirst," He cried in that dereliction of the Cross which

---

1　Isaias 42:4.　　　　2　Isaias 65:2.

was the most awful of His torments. He knows that its sense of its need of God, however dulled for awhile by the distractions of this life, becomes absolute and imperative beyond anything we can conceive, once the frontier is crossed and we enter upon the life beyond the grave. Only then can the soul enjoy perfect happiness, when in possession of the Object for which it was created, which fully occupies and wholly satisfies all its powers—that is, in the possession of God. Out of Him there is no happiness hereafter. And we must secure Him here, in time.

We are not to be Stoics or Puritans, without interest in the events of life, "without affection, without fidelity, without mercy"[1] a disposition intolerable to the ardent heart of St. Paul. A noble patriotism, an enthusiastic appreciation of the beautiful in nature and in art, a keen enjoyment of the innocent pleasures of life, a tender love of home and its ties, an intelligent response to the claims upon our interest in public or private life, a due insistence upon our rights in our relations with others—all this is consistent with St. John's teaching: "Love not the world nor the things which are in the world"[2], and St. Paul's: "This, therefore I say, brethren, the time is short: it remaineth that they that weep be as though they wept not; and they that rejoice as though they rejoiced not; and they that buy as though they possessed not; and they that use this world as though they used it not; for the fashion of this world passeth away."[3] Whilst it lasts for us we have to work out our salvation in it, using all things as means, not ends, as belonging to the stewardship for

1   Rom. 1:31.   2   1 John 2:15.   3   1 Cor. 7:29-31.

which we shall have to give an account, "good for the present necessity," as St. Paul says again[1], but not to be allowed to stifle in us the thirst for the good things to come. "Let temporal things serve thy need," À Kempis tells us, "but the eternal be the object of thy desire."

We have an example of a Christian of this stamp in that model layman, Blessed Thomas More. As husband, father, master, friend, subject, scholar and judge, he seems to us almost faultless. The present things of life might have entangled him, but his mind was too lofty to be enslaved by anything of this world. He knew how uncertain was his tenure of them and of life itself, and held them with a loose hand. And when the hour of trial came and he had to choose between these things and fidelity to his God, he let them go with a simplicity and a gladness that showed they had never been suffered to quench his thirst for "the strong, living God,"[2] and for the treasures that once secured, no man can take away.

"Blessed are they that hunger and thirst after justice for they shall have their fill."[3]

"My soul hath thirsted after the strong, living God."[4]

"For Thee my soul hath thirsted, for Thee my flesh, O how many ways!"[5]

"Give me the water of saving wisdom to drink."[6]

"Give me this water that I may not thirst."[7]

1　1 Cor. 7:26.　　　　2　Ps. 41:3.　　　　3　Matth 5:6.

4　Ps. 41:3.　　　　5　Ps. 62:2.　　　　6　Ecclus. 15:3.

7　John 4:15.

XLII

PLENTIFUL REDEMPTION

(Ps. 129)

"Then they shall see the Son of Man coming in a cloud with great power and majesty.... But when these things begin to come to pass look up, and lift up your heads because your redemption is at hand." (St. Luke 21:27-28.)

HAT a redemption that will be! Sin will have disappeared long ago with every shadow of weakness and defect. Purgatory's debt was paid at last, and to the eager waiting soul its Angel sped with the good tidings: "rise, make haste, my beautiful one and come."[1] "Put off the garment of thy mourning and affliction, and put on the beauty and honour of that everlasting glory which thou hast from God."[2] Perfect in its purity, all its powers quickened and strengthened by an intensity of life and energy compared with which the old life was but feebleness and torpor, it went forth from the prison-house, transformed, yet itself still, the character by which it was known on earth developed not destroyed, purged from every element of imperfection, but underlying

---

1   Cant. 2:10.   2   Baruch 5:1.

and permeating all the creations of grace, and giving it the distinctive holiness and attractiveness by which it is known among the Blessed.

But its companion the body—can this, too, expect redemption? Can we conceive of dishonour and ruin more irretrievable than that of the grave? Yet the hour will come when it will hear the voice of the Son of God, and come forth as a member of the body of Christ to take its share in His triumph. It has had its Purgatory, a humiliation so fundamental and so deep that only the Creator's hand could reach and rescue it. But "to the work of His hands He will reach out His right hand,"[1] and "it will live in His sight."[2] "It is sown in dishonour, it shall rise in glory. It is sown in weakness, it shall rise in power."[3] "I will redeem them from death."[4]

"Son of man, thinkest thou these bones shall live?"[5] There are men in our days who would have answered without hesitation: "Most certainly not, it would be contrary to all the laws of Nature and the principles of science." What said the wise prophet? "O Lord God, Thou knowest"[6]—that is: "All things depend on Thy Will, Nature has no other law, and must be prepared for any surprise if Thou but give the word." What a surprise awaits her on the Last Day:

> *Mors stupebit et natura*
> *Cum resurget creatura:*
>
> Nature shall see with dumb surprise
> The creature long consumed arise.

---

1   Job 14:15.   2   Osee 6:3.   3   1 Cor. 15:43.
4   Osee 13:14.   5   Ezechiel 37:3.   6   *ibid.*

For this restoration all the Saints wait and cry: "How long, O Lord, how long!" They ardently desire that redemption of the body, that reunion with the partner of their struggles and victories which so often was sacrificed to the interests of the soul. The Angel's trumpet at the Last Day will sound its hour of redemption, "for I know that my Redeemer liveth, and in the Last Day I shall rise out of the earth, and I shall be clothed again with my skin, and in my flesh I shall see my God, whom I myself shall see and my eyes shall behold and not another: this my hope is laid up in my bosom."[1]

"With Thee there is plentiful redemption," we say in hope each time the *De Profundis* recalls the humiliation of the grave. But Hope cannot forecast that complete rehabilitation which transcends all thought and desire, when "the enemy Death that is to be destroyed last"[2] shall be vanquished for ever, and all the elect shall rise in glory to meet Christ. The properties of a glorified body — immortality, impassibility, agility, clarity—as we see them in the Humanity of our Lord after the Resurrection, will be the sources of delight unimaginable now. No more need of wariness; Paradise, and no forbidden fruit; all the treasures of God thrown open to be enjoyed to the full, the liberty of the children of God complete!

Thus will the promise at Capharnaum be fulfilled: "He that eateth My flesh and drinketh My blood hath everlasting life and I will raise him up in the last Day."[3] In Holy Communion we receive the pledge of the eternal glory promised to the body; each time we communicate we

1 Job 19:25-27.   2 1 Cor. 15:26.   3 John 6:55.

renew that pledge and merit a new degree of likeness to our glorious Head. "It hath not yet appeared what we shall be, but we know that when He shall appear we shall be like to Him because we shall see Him as He is."[1]

"O happy fault, that deserved to have such a Redeemer!" is the marvellous cry of admiration and gratitude with which the Church, as a rule so calm in her utterances, welcomes her Lord back each year from the grave, "the first-fruits of them that sleep."[2] Well may she lay His members to their rest with all reverence, with chant, with incense, with the prayer of hope, and with the promise: "I am the Resurrection and the life, he that believeth in Me although he be dead shall live."[3]

In these days when faith in the resurrection of the body, like so many other fundamental truths, is losing its hold upon the minds of men, we must guard it jealously as the foundation that supports our faith and hope and the whole fabric of religion. In hours of sickness or weariness or combat when the flesh must be subdued by the spirit, let us repeat to ourselves: "I believe in the resurrection of the body." Let us promise it reward later for present restraint, and see it fail and decay, not as those who have no hope, but with the certainty that it will be restored to us endowed with new and wonderful powers in the resurrection.

> "Whoso laments, that we must doff this garb
> Of frail mortality, thenceforth to live
> Immortally above; he hath not seen
> The sweet refreshing of that heavenly shower.

*   *   *   *

---

1 1 John 3:2.   2 1 Cor. 15:20.   3 John 11:12.

Our shape, regarmented with glorious weeds,
Of saintly flesh, must, being thus entire,
Show yet more gracious.
Therefore shall increase
Whate'er, of light, gratuitous imparts
The Supreme Good; light ministering aid,
The better to disclose His glory,
…thus this circling sphere
Of splendour shall to view less radiant seem,
Than shall our fleshly robe, which yonder earth
Now covers. Nor will such excess of light
O'erpower us, in corporeal organs made
Firm, and susceptible of all delight."

    So ready and so cordial an "Amen"
Followed from either choir, as plainly spoke
Desire of their dead bodies; yet perchance
Not for themselves, but for their kindred dear,
Mothers and sires, and those whom best they loved
Ere they were made imperishable flame.

—*Paradise.* Canto XIV. Dante.

In view of its future glory, we shall treat the body
with reverence now, and discountenance in ourselves and
in others the love of display which disgraces too many
Christian women. Is it "the body of our lowness"[1] that
we see attracting to itself general attention in our streets,
and assembly rooms, and even in our churches; "daughters
decked out after the similitude of a temple"[2] to invite
admiration and worship! We may do our utmost to give
them credit for the best intentions like Judith, to whom
Scripture bears witness that "all this dressing up did not
proceed from sensuality but from virtue."[3] Yet we cannot
forget that virtue lies in the mean, that St. Paul would have
them "adorn themselves with modesty and sobriety…as

---

1   Philip. 3:21.   2   Ps. 143:12.   3   Judith 10:4.

it becometh women professing godliness,"[1] that Scripture bids us "turn away our face from a woman dressed up,"[2] and warns us that "the attire of the body shows what a man is."[3]

These bodies of ours are to be one day the admiration of the Angels and Saints; the gaze of the Immaculate is to rest lovingly upon them; they are to be objects of complacency to God Himself. In our treatment of them now, in the government of their craving for whatever ministers to their pleasure, we must hold them wisely in check and permit nothing that would be unworthy of or endanger their glory to come.

We have to bear in mind, too, that if it is to share the reward of the soul in eternity, the body must divide labour with it now. Eternal rest, which the Church desires for body and soul alike, supposes the present work of both. Killing time is not work; a round of endless amusement is not work; the selfishness that neglects its duties to others, is not work. The body must be taught that if it is the companion of the soul, it is still more its servant, and throughout the term of its service must be prepared to refrain from much and endure much in the interests of its lord. St. Bernard has a beautiful illustration of this. A certain prince being in exile took up his abode with a poor widow who in her poverty showed him all honour and reverence and went without many things that he might not want. Restored at length to his place in the kingdom of his father, he bethought him of her to whom he was so much beholden in the past, and begged that she might have remembrance and reward. "I beseech thee," so he prayed, "that this thy handmaid, who

---

1   1 Tim. 2:9-10.   2   Ecclus. 9:8.   3   Ecclus. 19:27.

for many years most patiently endured privation for my sake, may be sent for now to share my honours and my treasures."

Does my body realise its position as handmaid of my soul? Does it readily deny itself in the service of its prince, working hard now to deserve rest and glory hereafter? Of course the service will cost, but what of that? What if "the widow's tears run down the cheek"[1]—for a while? the day will come when they shall be dried and forgotten. Meantime we will say to her cheerily: "Work your work before the time and He will give you your reward in His time."[2]

---

1   Ecclus. 35:18.   2   Ecclus. 51:38.

XLIII

"THE DAY OF OUR LORD JESUS CHRIST"

(2 Cor. 1:14.)

HE minds of men are very variously affected by the influences under which they come. What will stir one to its depths and transform life for it, will have but a superficial effect upon another, and leave a third altogether unimpressed. But there is an influence none can wholly resist—the Saint, the sceptic, the reckless, the callous, none can face it without flinching. It is the thought of "the Great Day of the Almighty God,"[1] when "every man's work shall be manifest, for the day of the Lord shall declare it;"[2] "when God shall judge the secrets of men by Jesus Christ."[3]

Who can think of this Day without terror? St. Jerome could not. "Every night," he said, "when I lie down to rest, I think I hear the Angel's summons: 'Arise, ye dead, and come to Judgement!'" Whatever points to that Day affrights us. Events in which we think we discern "the beginnings of sorrows—earthquakes in divers places,

---

1 Apoc. 16:14. 2 1 Cor. 3:13. 3 Rom. 2:16.

the rising of nation against nation, wars, and rumours of wars," disquiet us doubly because we see in them forerunners of the end.

Our Lord Himself who is so loth to frighten, makes known to us the awful portents that are to herald the Last Day—"signs in the sun and in the moon and in the stars, the roaring of the sea and of the waves, men withering away for fear and expectation of what shall come upon the whole world."[1] The forces of nature that man has yoked to his service shall be in wild disarray; all he has counted as his own and built on for his enjoyment in an interminable future, shall suddenly fail him and disappear. "The heavens shall pass away with great violence, and the elements shall be melted with heat, and the earth and the works that are in it shall be burnt up."[2] With what terrific energy must that fire, the final instrument of God's justice, be endowed, when the very elements will be melted by its consuming heat! Can we conceive of destruction more complete, or of any feelings with regard to that Day but those of unmitigated terror!

Yet there is another aspect of it which we must not forget. Speaking to His Apostles our Lord gives this injunction: "When these things begin to come to pass, look up and lift up your heads because your redemption is at hand."[3] Self-forgetting always, His thoughts are still for us in that coming "day of the Lord," and as before His Ascension He bade His disciples be comforted because it was expedient for them that He should go, so when telling them of the Day when the Son of Man shall be seen coming in a cloud with great power and majesty, He

1 Luke 21:25-26.　　2 2 Peter 3:10.　　3 Luke 21:28.

says to them: "Look up and lift up your heads because your redemption is at hand."

Look up! The universal ruin which will fill with despair those whose all it has engulfed, will leave undismayed the hearts of the Saints who have kept themselves disengaged from the things of this world as having here no abiding city. The smoke of that holocaust which is the end of all earth's fair and costly things, will be to them but the incense announcing His approach on whom all their love and hopes are set, who is to them all in all.

Amid those scenes and sounds of terror, there will be His word to them from the glowing heavens, His favorite word to His own: "Fear not, it is I. Behold My hands and My feet and see that it is I Myself." "Fear not you," the Angel said to the women at the Sepulchre, "for I know that you seek Jesus who was crucified." And all these with upturned faces have sought Him through the dimness and perplexities of the past, have followed where Faith led, and refused to be lured aside by the false lights of so-called advanced thought, and theories that would have emancipated them from the subjection of Faith. There were difficulties for them as for others; they could not understand but they believed and they hoped; in the darkness they clung to the hand of the Church and she has brought them safe—to this! They knew whom they had believed and were certain He was able to keep that which they had committed to Him against this Day. They sought Jesus who was crucified, they carried their cross after Him, and that cross is now their salvation. Resplendent with glory it appears in the heavens, and lo! on the forehead of all these to the right, appears that saving sign.

They are His, He has come for them, they are to share His triumph—why should they not rejoice! Amidst the awful confusion of that Day when "the stars shall be falling down, and the powers that are in heaven shall be moved, He shall send His Angels and shall gather together His elect from the four winds, from the uttermost part of the earth to the uttermost part of heaven."[1] What tenderness there is in these, His own words of reassurance! Others are to be summoned to Judgement, "the elect and faithful"[2] are to be gathered together by Angels and brought to Him. Not one shall be forgotten; however scattered, they shall be brought together; however lowly, they are His and He in His glory will remember and send for them. Lord, remember me when Thou shalt come into Thy Kingdom!

But there is a stronger, higher cause for rejoicing yet. He who taught us to say: "Thy Kingdom come!" would have us share His desire for the coming of that Day when He shall "deliver up the Kingdom to the Father…that God may be all in all."[3] Must we not be glad for His sake, glad for His triumph, glad to see all things under His feet?[4] "Father," He prayed as He left this world, "I will that where I am they also whom Thou hast given Me may be with Me that they may see My glory."[5] Holy Job amid the dimness of heathendom longed for that sight. David cried out: "I shall be satisfied when Thy glory shall appear."[6] Have we less reason to rejoice than these?

---

1   Mark 13:25, 27.   2   Apoc. 17:14.   3   1 Cor. 15:24, 28.
4   1 Cor. 15:26.   5   John 17:24.   6   Ps. 16:15.

"The Son of Man shall come in His majesty and all the Angels with Him, and shall sit upon the seat of His majesty. And all nations shall be gathered together before Him."[1] Shall we not "be glad and rejoice when the marriage of the Lamb is come,[2] and the Church which has prepared herself is there, gathered together unto Him,"[3] perfected at last, no longer Suffering and Militant but all Triumphant, "a glorious Church without spot or wrinkle,"[4] "clothed with fine linen glittering and white, the bride of the Lamb"?[5]

What joy there shall be in that "day of the Lord "when the work of "everyone that loveth and maketh a lie"[6] shall be brought to naught, and Truth—Truth prevail at last! When there shall be but one standard of judgement and of goodness—His Judgement and His Will; when the secrets of His Providence shall be made known for the adoration and admiration of all men; when His government of the world and His dealings with each and every soul shall be justified in the sight of all, and the confidence and "the patience of the Saints"[7] have their reward! At the thought of that Day our hearts expand with a loyalty that leaves no room for self-seeking, with that pride in Him which is the keynote of the exultation of the Saints: "We give Thee thanks, O Lord God Almighty, who art and who wast and who art to come: because Thou hast taken to Thee Thy great power and Thou hast reigned."[8] "Salvation to our God who sitteth upon the throne and to

---

1   Matth. 25:31-32.   2   Apoc. 19:7.   3   2 Thess. 2:1.
4   Ephes. 5:21.   5   Apoc. 19:8, 21:9.   6   Apoc. 22:15.
7   Apoc. 14:12.   8   Apoc. 11:17.

the Lamb…Amen. Benediction and glory, and wisdom and thanksgiving, honour and power, and strength to our God for ever and ever. Amen."[1]

There is thus a twofold expectation with which we look forward to this "Day of the Lord." We await it with dread for it is the "day of wrath,"[2] but also with joy and confidence for it is "the day of redemption,"[3] "the day of our Lord Jesus Christ,"[4] "when He shall come to be glorified in His Saints and to be made wonderful in all them who have believed."[5]

This "day of Christ" was continually in the heart and on the lips of St. Paul. He speaks of it again and again to his beloved Philippians.[6] To Timothy he merely says, "in that day," "against that day,"[7] as reference sufficient to what was constantly in the minds of both.

In his own affectionate way he uses this "waiting for the manifestation of our Lord Jesus Christ"[8] as a powerful incentive to fervour and perseverance: "We beseech you, brethren, by the coming of our Lord Jesus Christ and of our gathering together unto Him…"[9] The day of the Lord shall come as a thief in the night. But the children of light and children of the day are always to rejoice, to pray without ceasing, in all things to give thanks that their whole spirit and soul and body may be preserved blameless in the coming of our Lord Jesus Christ.[10]

In St. Peter, too, we see the same eager longing for a Day whose terrors he depicts in words unsurpassed for

1   Apoc. 7:10, 12.   2   Rom. 2:5.   3   Ephes. 4:30.
4   2 Cor. 1:14.   5   2 Thess. 1:10.   6   Phil. 1:6.
7   2 Tim. 1:12, 4:8.   8   1 Cor. 1:7.   9   2 Thess. 2:1.
10   1 Thess. 5:23.

their appalling force: "Looking for and hasting unto the coming of the day of the Lord by which the heavens being on fire shall be dissolved and the elements shall melt in the burning heat."[1]

So habitually did the first faithful live in expectation of the Second Coming of Christ, that they came to look upon it as immediate. It was an expectancy that thrilled the Church for centuries, and served to sustain her amid the fierceness of the persecution and dangers by which she was assailed. It enabled Christians to withstand the seduction of a corrupt pagan society; it supported the martyrs in their torments; it inspired the detachment of the anchorets who fled the world's business, and honours and pleasures altogether lest they should be found unprepared at the Lord's Coming.

Why should not the same motive have force with us in our very different vocations? Shall Job look forward with such steadfast trust and desire to beholding his Redeemer at the Last Day, and we see it approaching with no feelings but dread? The remembrance of it in the spirit of the early Church would keep up in our hearts that sense of fellowship with Christ, that personal love of Him, of desire for His glory, of union with Him in mind and heart and interests which St. Paul desires for us. It would keep our hearts pure, and peaceful, and detached, unworldly in the midst of worldliness, unspotted amid corruption, undismayed at the changes and troubles of this passing life. Because "we have not here a lasting city," we shall be able to part without repining with the things of this

1   2 Peter 3:12.

world. Because we love Christ above all things we shall desire to see His glory and to be with Him.

And—we shall heed His word of warning, "*Watch! Watch ye therefore, praying at all times, that you may be accounted worthy to escape all these things that are to come, and to stand before the Son of Man.*[1] *And what I say to you I say to all—Watch!*"

---

1 Luke 21:36.

XLIV

ST. MARY MAGDALEN

HERE and how did He first cross her path? Was it the majesty of His bearing, the glance of His eye, the tone of His voice, the word that fell from His lips, that captivated her and made her His for ever? We are not told. But we know it was the divine influence acting through these channels, the special ray of grace destined for her from all eternity, that enlightened, subdued, and drew her powerfully to Him and secured to Him for ever all the devotedness of that ardent heart.

There is consolation here for us who have not yet seen Him. We shall never in this life meet Him like Mary Magdalen. But for us, too, He has special graces prepared from eternity, and sent when their hour is come through the circumstances of our lives. In a Communion, in a book taken up at an odd moment, in a chance conversation, Christ, bringing with Him the grace of our life, may come. "But not," someone will say, "with the attractiveness, the overmastering charm with which He came to her."

And what of that! Our Lord will not indeed come visibly and suddenly into our life as into hers and change the face of all things to us. But if we will heed His invitation and work with His grace, He will make Himself more and more to us day by day, and change us from what we are to what He desires to see us.

God has a special service for each one of us. To this end He gives graces specially adapted thereto—these, not those. We must not covet the portion of another whose task is different, but lay hold on our own grace and work it diligently. If He puts the hammer and plane into our hands, we must not want the palette or the burin. If our sphere of labour is plainly within the walls of our home, we must not pine for the hospital or the slums. The reward we want from Him when our work is done must be for the work He gives us to do. His estimate of its worth will not be determined by the judgements of men. The weights of the sanctuary are utterly different from the valuations of earth. Before Him, service is measured, not by its outward seeming, but by the intention of the will. The coster's and the charwoman's is more prized than the politician's and the preacher's if the motive that inspires it be worthier— that is, more purely directed to His service and praise.

Why waste our time, then, in fretting for fields of labour which are beyond our reach! Surely our Master may put us where He will. And when we know that the spot assigned to us to tend is chosen in view of our special aptitudes and reward, how is it we are so perverse as to desire anything different?

So with our temperament and surroundings and gifts. If we have not the ardour of Magdalen, or been called to the Feet of Christ Himself for our absolution, He will not expect from us what He looked for from her. But He will and does expect at our hands the service for which our capabilities and the daily current of our lives furnish the opportunities. It was not to the ten talents or to the four that the praise: "Well done, good and faithful servant," was given, but to the fidelity that had multiplied in each case the Master's trust.

"Take what is thine and go thy way," our Lord says to us lovingly, when we look discontentedly at our own penny and enviously at another's. He does not ask us to use another's grace and bring to Him another's work for reward. By the way, how many of the Saints, had they been so minded, might have desired our graces and opportunities! Instead of coveting what has not been given us, let us like them put to profit our own stock, fight our own difficulties, make up our own crown.

We notice, perhaps, that it is the marvellous and the exceptional in the Saints that we are wont to envy. We do not find ourselves sighing after the years of rigorous penance and lonely prayer when He was gone, by which Magdalen kept her heart for Him who had won it, and made reparation for the past. It is the sweets of God's consolations that we want; not further opportunities of service, but pleasant pastures for our own delectation. Does this look quite like the self-forgetfulness that might entitle us to special favour!

Magdalen had her singular graces and reward. Ours, too, are singular, unlike those of any other, entitling us to a special place in His Heart whom, with her, we love to call in love and trust "*Rabboni.*" Can we desire anything more or better?

XLV

TRUST

"Thy sins are forgiven thee, go in peace." (St. Luke 7:48-50.)

OW strangely timorous are these poor hearts of ours! Do what He will, God cannot bring us to confide in Him as we ought. In spite of the tenderest words and deeds and promises by which He seeks to win us, we seem to have a lurking suspicion that He cannot really care for us and wish us well. Worst of all, it is in the matter most vital to us, sin and its forgiveness, that our mistrust reaches its height. We think it safer to doubt God's pardon than to take His word for it. He says to us: "Go in peace," and we remain troubled. We are like frightened children who have been cruelly treated and are dazed and bewildered when they come into kind hands. For a time tender words and ways puzzle instead of reassuring them. But, unlike the children, some of us remain distrustful to the end. Our Father's love and goodness has never been able to inspire the confidence He asks and prizes.

We say we cannot help ourselves, we are made that way. This is surely a mistake; we can help ourselves greatly by the thoughtful pondering of the words and ways by which He shows us that He means us to take Him at His word. Those who knew Him best during His life on earth never dreamed of believing that penitence, to be sincere and seemly, must be downhearted and inert. Magdalen after her absolution was the constant companion of Mary Immaculate and stood by her side beneath the Cross. After his fall and forgiveness, Peter's love showed the same ardour and venturesomeness that had characterised it before.

And look at the Prodigal Son, the model penitent set before us by Our Lord Himself. He knew his father's heart or he would never have gone home at all, yet there may well have been misgivings on the way. But when he fell on his knees before him and felt the pressure of the arms round his neck, and the wet tears on his cheek, and knew from the tender words that he was forgiven *quite*, and taken back to his home not as a servant but as a son—did he think propriety required him to question these evidences of love and to show himself downcast and dissatisfied?

Oh, that we were like that poor boy after his return! That we went home with our Father grateful and happy, contented—more than contented with all He had done for us. But we go on doubting and sulking, saying we are unlike Magdalen and Peter who had their forgiveness from the lips of Christ Himself. No such comforting assurance has been given *us*. Nor will it be given if we wait till doomsday. Nor has it been given to the millions upon millions who, trusting in the promise, "he that heareth you heareth Me, whose sins you shall forgive they are forgiven," have knelt at the feet of Christ in the confessionals of the Church, and gone away—in peace.

If we will continue sullen and querulous, there is no help for it, but at least let us be honest enough to own that the fault is our own, that the Almighty God can do no more for us, and that the thankfulness and happy trust which are so beautiful a part of real penitence are conspicuously absent from our own.

XLVI

RUNNING

"I, therefore, so run not as at an uncertainty." (1 Cor. 9:26.)

HIS, the most simple, unlettered child of the Church may say with fullest confidence. Whilst "the wise and prudent" are crying out that there is no certainty for us except in the evidence of the senses— where the commonest juggler and ventriloquist will tell us it certainly *is not*—"the little ones" are walking on securely amidst spiritual realities as far above the things of sense as the soul is above the body.

Nay, they do more than walk, they run. Now, running implies such confidence in the path that the whole attention can be fixed on the goal, such delight in the prospect that there is no temptation to tarry by the way, such inward vigour, that the limbs find pleasure in putting out their strength, such preparation and facilities of the road, that it is neither too stony nor too steep.

Happy children of the Catholic Church! for this is, or may be, the lot of every one of them. Like the great Apostle, they run at no uncertainty. Many an honest seeker spends the better part of life in painful search for his road, whilst they, from early dawn, perhaps, have had their feet firmly set therein. "The faith once delivered to the Saints" is passed down to them as a torch on a perilous path. It has guided multitudes of their brethren gone on before, and brought them safe to their Home; it will do the like for all those who grasp it firmly and walk by its light. Its ray falls steadily on the things of time, that the traveller may not be lured from his path by the fascination of passing charms; it shows the Home on the mountain, so bright, so inviting, that the weary step quickens once more into a run.

With such light and help, with such welcome awaiting us, how is it we do not hasten forward one and all! There is enough, there is everything to make us run—not as at an uncertainty, but to the reward promised us on the word of God, to the Kingdom prepared for us from the foundation of the world. The goal of the journey is no matter for indifference, nor for resignation, but for burning desire, and steady effort, and faithful perseverance to the end. We must not crawl to it, nor even hasten—*but run.*

XLVII

"LORD, TEACH US TO PRAY"

S T. ALPHONSUS LIGOURI, considering the vast multitude assembled in the valley of Jehoshaphat at the Last Day, awaiting the coming of the Judge, asks what has divided them into those two ranks which can never again be united. On the right, is the dazzling company of those who stand with lifted heads and longing hearts because their Redemption is at hand. Herded together on the left, is the appalling multitude of those on whom irreparable ruin has come.

What is the cause of the sundering of this vast gathering? Why is it that these have saved and those have lost their souls? Is it that some have inherited a temperament naturally prone to virtue and others to vice? That the good education and home influences here have been wanting there? That one set has been shielded from temptations to which others have been exposed? That there have been no grievous and repeated falls on one side, and many on the other?

No, none of these things is the cause of the difference to which their lives have brought them. On both sides there have been good homes and bad, good example and bad, violent temptations, and grand opportunities. By the force of external circumstances alone, no man stands or falls, but by the way he exerts his free-will upon them and uses or neglects the help of prayer.

By prayer those on the right have put to profit the good in themselves and in their surroundings, and neutralised the evil. By neglect of prayer those on the left have wasted their advantages and fallen victims to their corrupt inclinations.

Here is the secret: what must be our petition when we learn it? Surely—"Lord, teach us to pray, and help us to persevere in humble fervent prayer to the end!"

XLVIII

OUR ANGEL GUARDIAN

"What can we give him sufficient for these things?" (Tobias 12:3.)

THOSE who have lived with Saints tell us that nearness to them in time of prayer has a wonderful power of enkindling fervour. We live all our life long in close companionship with an Angel of God. What if we were to remember his presence more in time of prayer, to draw closer to him then, that from his glowing ardour we might inflame our own cold hearts!

And would it be doing too much by way of return for his untiring devotion to us, if we were sometimes to return thanks to God in his behalf, and offer him our congratulations as we are wont to do to our friends of earth?

My God, I thank Thee for the glorious spirit that, straight from Thy immediate Presence, and the sight of Thy unveiled Face, is sent to minister to me. I thank and bless Thee for his creation, for the Divine complacency that from all eternity has rested on him, for his spotless innocence that no breath of sin has ever tarnished, for his perfect beauty, and for that special excellence which makes him singularly acceptable to Thee and beloved.

I thank Thee for his loyalty to Thee when so many of his companions fell away, for the eternal happiness then assured to him, that no further trial can ever endanger, that unabating shall be his for ever.

I thank Thee, that because of some peculiar fitness, known to Thee, he and no other has been Thy choice for me, to be my guardian and companion through life. I thank and bless Thee for all the help and grace which in time of need his prayer has won for me, for all the graces yet in store for me, and the happy death his prayer will secure to me, the welcome Thou wilt give us both when he brings me to Thee for Judgement, the help on earth he will procure for me and bring me in Purgatory, the joy with which he will come for me when my time has come, the contentment with which he will present me purified and perfected before Thy Face.

O my Lord, to me hidden, to him unveiled, reward him, I beseech Thee, as Thou knowest how, for his faithful love and care of me, and make me draw from his constant nearness to me, especially in time of prayer, the reverence and fervour in which I am so sadly wanting.

Blessed spirit, nearest and dearest to me of the citizens of Heaven, bring me safely to my place before the Throne of God where I may praise Him with thee for ever. And help me to begin now what is to be my occupation for eternity. Help me in prayer to realise thy nearness; inspire me with thy reverence for the God of Heaven and earth here truly present; inflame me with thy burning love of Him; unite my adoration with thine; let me thank Him with thee for benefits which I appreciate so poorly though they cost the blood of God to purchase. Share with me thy vehement desires for His glory, thy swiftness in His service, thy zeal for His little ones, the vigilance, patience and love with which thou dost guard and minister to them.

Teach me, my elder brother, to do our Father's Will as It is done in Heaven, without misgiving, without delay, with the delight that comes of absolute loyalty and perfect trust. Get me deeper, more lively faith in the Real Presence on the altar, known by sight to thee, by faith to me. How different is my faith to that of the Saints! As they knelt before the altar by the side of their Guardian Angels, what wonderful worship, what acceptable prayer and praise went up to God. My cold distracted prayer is surely displeasure and distress to thee. Help me to a converse with God more like to thine. Pray for this, that I may be a less unworthy companion for thee when we come together before the altar to speak to thy God and mine.

XLIX

"THE SERPENT DECEIVED ME"

(Gen. 3:13.)

"To this end he came to thee that he might deceive thee."
(2 Kings 3:25.)

ILLUSIONS serve our enemy's purpose better in the long run than temptation. Evil in itself is unattractive; we are conscious of yielding to it for the bait it offers to passion and against the calm judgement of reason. We arm ourselves against it by prayer and the Sacraments. When we conquer, we know there is laid up for us the reward of those who have "striven lawfully." When we fall, the shock rouses us, humbles us and makes us more wary for the future. So great, indeed, are the advantages to be derived from temptation, that the Scripture seems to make little account of virtue as yet untested: "What doth he know that hath not been tried?"[1] "Because thou wast acceptable to God it was necessary that temptation should prove thee."[2] We see in effect that all God's rational creatures who have come to the use of reason have had to do battle to win the victor's crown.

---

1 Ecclus. 34:9.   2 Tobias 12:13.

Temptation, inasmuch as it is a solicitation to evil, is simply hateful, but at least it has the merit of coming to us with its evil countenance unveiled. It is otherwise with illusion, the harm that insinuates itself under the appearance of good. This does not frighten us, we go with it unsuspectingly, we defend it, not only to others but to our own conscience.

The state of our health requires all these little indulgences; prevention is better than cure. It is useful to read such and such objectionable books that we may know what is to be said on the other side and be able to help others. Life is not meant to be a perpetual strain, "reasonable service" is all that is required of us; prayer, self-denial, almsgiving, must be understood rationally, and not be allowed to interfere with our social duties, and the exigencies of our position. After all, freedom from mortal sin is all that is needed to get to Heaven; the Church herself does not exact more than the Sacraments once a year. Anything more is very well for those who feel called to it, but extremes are always dangerous, and really the eccentricities of pious people do not encourage one to follow in their steps. What harm if the day does go in novel reading, dressing, visits, amusement! There is nothing wrong in these things, no hard and fast line can be drawn, the rush of life in these days and the necessity of doing as others do, obliges one to be content with little in the way of Church going. As to charities, it is simply impossible to meet the incessant calls thrust upon one. Charity begins at home, one's family has the first claim; duty to those about us forbids us to think of coming into contact with the poor in their unsanitary homes, or of that expenditure of time and talent in their service which those more fortunately situated than ourselves are able to indulge in.

Besides this class of illusions—too patent, perhaps, to ensnare souls with any degree of earnestness in the service of God—there are others, which fasten on to that very earnestness like parasites on to a fruitful tree.

There is the perpetual fear about past confessions with which some are haunted, with the result that through anxiety for the past, the present and the future are neglected, hope and courage die down, with all energy for the work of self-conquest and of self-sacrifice in the service of souls.

Along with this pusillanimity, goes the presumption that makes one prefer one's own judgement to one's confessor's, and to suppose one's spiritual condition to be so singular that no other case presents a parallel to it, the moral theology of the Church has no provision for it, her ministers one and all have no experience or comprehension of it. Whence it follows, that as in matters of salvation we must be on the safe side always, private judgement is the only guidance we can accept in a case we alone understand. The Church's teaching that safety is only secured by obedience manifestly does not apply to us and must be ignored. Life, and the patience of our so-called guides must be spent in the perpetual rehearsal of the same old story and in the attempt on our part to prove how inadequate is their theological training to reassure a soul involved in such mystery as ours. Holy Scripture describes our frame of mind: "Thy wisdom and thy knowledge, this hath deceived thee. And thou hast said in thy heart: I am, and besides me there is no other."[1]

Again, there is the further presumption of maintaining our own opinion against the teaching of the Vicar of Christ in the matter of frequent Communion. He says that freedom from conscious mortal sin and a right intention is sufficient for a good and fruitful Communion; that our Lord desires to give Himself to us frequently and even daily, and that, provided we bring these necessary dispositions, no one is to deter us from daily Communion.

We say that, allowing this to be true in the main, it jars upon our views of what the exalted nature of the Sacrament exacts of us. At any rate, the meagre dispositions required of others would not suffice to make daily approach to Christ on our part acceptable either to Him or to ourselves. More must surely be demanded *of us.* And so, whilst those around us, relying simply on the Church's teaching, and thankful for the wondrous provision made by the goodness of God for these difficult days of ours, throng up to the altar rails and, like Zaccheus of old, "receive Him with joy," we, in our superior light, look on from behind, and wait the time when, with the Jansenists, we shall judge our dispositions sufficiently befitting the Most Holy Sacrament to permit us to approach ourselves.

These are but samples of the illusions with which the enemy of souls blinds many who might be superb servants of God. Looking at it honestly, and in the case of others, we see the peril of illusion in the concerns of the soul. Temptation, open and straightforward, is a foe less difficult

---

1   Isaias 47:10.

to meet and less dangerous. So far from fostering pride, it humbles us and makes us fly fervently and trustfully to God. But illusion is the very hotbed of pride. It enables us calmly to set our own judgement above the highest authority on earth, and without misgiving to accept the risk of so doing; to be proof against the infallible voice and the earnest solicitations of the Shepherd and Teacher of all the faithful and to the desires of God Himself. Well may the Church bid us pray:

"From the illusions and temptations of the devil, O Lord, deliver us!"

L

O SACRUM CONVIVIUM

"Thou didst feed Thy people with the food of Angels, and gavest them bread from heaven, prepared without labour; having in it all that is delicious, and the sweetness of every taste." (Wisd. 16:20.)

HE *food of Angels*—satisfying to the full those noble spirits, all but infinite in number and variety and capacity for knowledge and for love. Who are we that their food, the bread of Heaven, should be ours also?

Prepared without labour—on our part but not on His who gives it to us. From all eternity, Bethlehem, and Nazareth, and the Supper Room stood out clear and distinct in the mind of God; my Communion of tomorrow was foreseen, my Food prepared. All His Life long, Jesus desired with desire the hour when He should give Himself to me as my food. He knows the value of my soul, its natural dignity as an immortal spirit, created by God and in the image and likeness of God; its supernatural dignity as a child of God, redeemed with the blood of God, destined to share for eternity the happiness of God Himself. And He judges that for a creature so noble, so beloved, the Bread of Angels is the meetest rood. They feed indeed in a happier manner,[1] but the Food is the same for those elder sons of God and for us whom the Man-God is not ashamed to call His brethren.

He knows that between our place of exile and the Heavenly City for which we are bound, there are slippery paths and pitfalls, perils of every kind which would certainly be our destruction were we not protected and fortified from above. He must provide a sustenance that will not only repair our daily losses, but strengthen us against every danger, make us a match for any enemy, satisfy, as far as may be here below, the craving of the soul. What could this be but Himself?

O Heavenly Food, having in thee all that is delicious and the sweetness of every taste, let me so hunger after thee as to be forced to make thee my daily bread. O living Bread, that hast come down from Heaven to give life to the world, unworthy as I am to receive thee, I will come and come often, that I may abide in thee and thou in me; that I may live by thee, and be raised up by thee to everlasting life at the Last Day.

---

1   *Imit.*, Bk. 4, Ch. 2.

L I

PATIENCE

"I know thy works, and thy labour, and thy patience." (Apoc. 2:2.)

AVE we ever noticed the stress which throughout the Scriptures God lays on patience? He is patient, we are told, because He is eternal. To us who are but of yesterday, here today and gone tomorrow, patience comes with difficulty and not without long practice. And because it is of all things necessary for us, He urges us to the acquisition of it and marks His appreciation of it.

The writers of the Old Testament often speak of the patience of God. Holy Job was given as a model of patience to all time. Our Lord in His Passion was "led as a sheep to the slaughter";[1] "when He was reviled He did not revile, when He suffered He threatened not."[2]

St. Paul in almost all his Epistles, St. Peter, St. James, St. John in the Apocalypse, untiringly exhort to patience. And, indeed, it must have seemed the one thing necessary in those days of fierce persecution of the infant Church: "Hold fast that which thou hast that no man take thy

---

1   Isaias 53:7.   2   1 Peter 2:23.

crown,"[1] was an injunction continually needed by the first sorely tried followers of our Lord.

But is it less necessary now? Is fortitude less called for in our days? The nature of the trial has changed, but indifferentism, materialism, worldliness, human respect, are tyrants with whom we can no more compound than could the early Christians with the exactions of the Roman Emperors—if we would save our souls.

Patience is needed, to resist the constant pressure upon us of these forces from without, and of that traitor within who is always ready to make common cause with them. It is needed, too, in the trials of every kind with which life abounds, some crushing by their weight and suddenness, others chafing by their persistent friction; now severe pain, physical or mental, now the monotony of our daily task, the weariness of uncongenial work or surroundings, the failure of generous endeavour, the apathy or mistakes of friends—and worse still, our own—the odds against us in the upholding of right principles, the inadequacy of effort to stem the torrent of evil in any direction, or to meet the crying needs on every side. How much there is to bring home to us the need of the counsel which runs through Holy Scripture from beginning to end:

"Wait on God with patience, join thyself to God and endure."[2]

"The patient man is better than the valiant."[3]

"Take all that shall be brought upon thee, and in thy sorrow endure, and in thy humiliation keep patience."[4]

---

1 Apoc. 3:11. 2 Ecclus. 2:23. 3 Prov. 16:32.
4 Ecclus. 2:4.

"Expect the Lord, do manfully, and let thy heart take courage, and wait thou for the Lord."[1]

"If He delay wait for Him, for He will surely come and will not be slack."[2]

"Blessed are all they that wait for Him."[3]

"For they shall not be confounded that wait for Him."[4]

One reason why many give up the service of God altogether, and many more give up anything like a generous service, is because they have not the courage and humility to be patient with the poor result of their efforts at self-conquest. If they could bring themselves into shape by a few fierce blows, they would strike hard and have done with it. But the work is not to be dispatched in this fashion any more than a perfect head can be brought out of the marble by a few strokes. There must be daily, patient, toil—chiselling, filing, polishing, a less acute angle here, a trifle more rounding there. Such little, little things—and little too, to show for it. People who understand nothing of the sculptor's art come in and out and wonder what he has been doing all these weeks; they see no change. But let a connoisseur or a fellow worker come in—and how his eye lights up! He sees how much has been done, how the likeness is coming out. Everyone will see and praise by and by. But to his eye there is beauty even at this stage, in spite of all the roughness. Finish will come later; he can wait for that. But his admiration and congratulation are ready now.

---

1 Ps. 26:14.   2 Hab. 2:3.   3 Isaias 30:18.
4 Isaias 49:23.

So are our Lord's. He will not wait till He takes the finished work from us at the end, to say: "Well done!" He is behind us now as we toil on day after day. He is looking over our shoulder, watching every effort, often approving when others blame, noting with pleasure the likeness to Himself coming out beneath the patient endeavour helped by His grace.

We must not look for sudden transformations like St. Paul's on the road to Damascus. Our work, like that of almost every Saint, is to be a gradual one, the work of our life. Is this discouraging? But life is given us for this, it is the workshop, not the gallery. If "the Lord patiently expecteth,"[1] surely we may have patience with ourselves. We may and we must. "Patience is necessary for you," says St. Paul.[2] Yes truly, for without patience, perseverance will fail, the grace on which our eternity depends.

Prayer, and the Sacraments, and effort, may for a time appear to make little difference; we must go on in patience and in trust. A stage will come when every touch will tell, when the patient elaboration of details will result in the perfection of the whole, and God's ideal will be realised at last. "Let us humbly wait for His consolation."[3] "Stay patiently awhile, and thou shalt see His great power."[4]

So is it in the order of nature, "first the blade, then the ear, afterwards the full corn in the ear."[5] "Be patient, therefore, brethren," says St. James, "behold the husbandman waiteth for the precious fruit of the earth, patiently bearing till he receive the early and the latter

---

1 2 Mach. 6:14.   2   Heb. 10:36.   3   Judith 8:20.
4 2 Mach. 7:17.   5   Mark 4:28.

rain. Be you, therefore, also patient and strengthen your hearts."[1]

It is remarkable that our Lord Himself did not choose always to effect an instantaneous cure. When the blind man of Bethsaida was asked if he saw anything, he answered: "I see men as it were trees, walking." Yet the wonderworking hands had touched his eyes. "After that again He laid His hands upon his eyes, and he began to see, and was restored so that he saw all things clearly."[2]

This is, indeed, the only recorded instance of a gradual restoration among the cures wrought by our Lord. But it represents the usual working of grace in our souls, a dispensation whose value in safeguarding humility, and fostering patience and fortitude, a habit of prayer, courage and perseverance, is not hard to see.

But whilst we bear in mind that grace, like nature, works slowly and almost imperceptibly, we must not therefore conclude that a snail's pace is all that should be expected of us in the way of advance, and that no blame attaches to us if we are much as we were years ago. More heart in our spiritual concerns, better preparation for prayer and the Sacraments would doubtless prepare the way for grace and enable it to do greater things for us. "Do what is in thy power," À Kempis tells us, "and God will be with thy good will."

A daily exercise in the laborious work of self-training and self-sacrifice, is the cheerful acceptance of the ups and downs of daily life.

---

1   James 5:7-8.   2   Mark 8:25.

How far this has taken many a valiant soul, whose circumstances seemed hopelessly commonplace, the Last Day will reveal. Heroism is not the monopoly of the Martyrs. Everywhere there are sufferings that can be borne heroically for Christ; what is wanting is the effort to turn them to profit.

> Blessed are those who die for God,
>   And earn the Martyr's crown of light—
> Yet he who lives for God may be
>   A greater conqueror in His sight.[1]

Many motives may help us here. In pain of mind we may bring to remembrance the agony and desolation of our Lord in the Garden and on the Cross; in pain of body, the thorn-crowned Head, or the Five Wounds.

Or we may take the encouragement furnished by our Lord Himself in the thought: "Your Father knoweth."[2]

"*I know thy works and thy labour.*—What if the faithful discharge of little duties is taken for granted and passed by unappreciated by others—*I know.* The effort to be patient and cheerful at monotonous work, the suppression of unkind judgements and hasty words, the surrender of private wishes that another's may prevail, the peaceful acceptance of dryness in prayer and Communion, the weary waiting for the fulfilment of good desires, the patience and perseverance when the prayer of years seems to go unanswered—*all this, I know.*"

Oh yes, when hope and courage are at their lowest, and the irksomeness of effort presses heaviest, what comfort

---

1 *Maximus*, Adelaide Proctor.   2 Matth. 6:8.

and strength there is in the thought that our Father knows it all!

I know thy patience. Patience is harder than the most laborious work. We tire so soon. We want to see results at once. To hold on in spite of monotony and failure, and no seeming progress, is hard even to the bravest. But see what account He makes of it all:

"*I know thy works and thy labour and thy patience.* And thou hast endured for My Name and hast not fainted. Be thou faithful unto death, and I will give thee the crown of life….Behold I come quickly and My reward is with Me.[1] I am thy protector and thy reward exceeding great."[2]

---

1   Apoc 22:16.   2   Gen. 15:1.

L I I

SURSUM CORDA!

I F I have acquired a property in a distant country, I must needs, like the man in the Gospel, go to see it. Circumstances may perhaps prevent my starting at once, but I am impatient to be off; meanwhile delay only whets desire and stimulates imagination. I find myself at free moments, indeed at all times, conjuring up pictures, making plans, building castles of all shapes and dimensions. If the climate and productions of the country are different from those at home, if it is a fair land with unlimited resources, fancy simply runs riot. I am observed to be frequently abstracted, my thoughts evidently far away; my conversation, in spite of myself, betrays me. In short, though I cannot be said to neglect my present duties, I live in the future, a fact which, under the circumstances, is considered not only excusable but inevitable. In a few years, people say, my home will be there, how can I be otherwise than absorbed in the prospect and in preparation.

Yes; thus it would certainly be were there question of a little bit of this poor world. Mind and heart would be travelling perpetually to that land beyond the sea, and effort would be necessary to concentrate my thoughts sufficiently on actual work at home. But when my possession is—not a few acres here for the space of this passing life, but the inheritance secured to me by my Baptism, an "inheritance incorruptible reserved in Heaven,"[1] a Kingdom prepared for me from the foundation of the world, a Land fair beyond all conception, whose delights "eye hath not seen, nor ear heard, nor heart conceived,"—it is a different case. Where is my enthusiasm now? When do my words, my unworldly thoughts and ways betray me and show that I feel I have not here a lasting city and that I seek one that is to come; that the sense of exile weighs upon me; that I listen longingly for the invitation: "Arise, make haste and come, for winter is now past, the rain is over and gone, the flowers have appeared in our land…arise and come"?[2]

If it is not thus with me, how can so strange a fact be explained? for, supposing my faith to be what it should be, such causes as forgetfulness, business, the pressure of daily cares, and the like, would be obviously inadequate. But *is* my faith what it should be: not only firm but lively, influencing my thoughts, words, and acts? I notice this peculiarity about my thoughts. Of "the Four Last Things to be ever remembered" I rarely think at all. If at distant intervals I do advert to any, it is either to the two that pass swiftly never to return, or to that terrible one, the resource in moments of strong temptation. But as to the fourth, which is my portion for ever, my eternal dwelling-place, the reward I am living to secure, this hardly ever comes to mind. I almost look upon it as a fairy land,

---

1   1 Peter 1:4.   2   Cant. 2:10-11, 13.

beautiful but unreal, no motive, therefore, for action, no encouragement in time of trial, no fact having any practical bearing on my life.

Yet what should interest and influence me like the thought of Heaven! In cases of threatened heart failure we keep at hand remedies which stimulate its action and reinforce its vitality. Why not, in hours of weariness and heartsinking, turn to the thought of our Eternal Home as a restorative and refreshment! We know enough of its joys to make the remembrance of them a powerful stimulant to hope and to effort. Let us take a few of these joys and dwell thoughtfully on them one by one.

Joy in the sense of Safety. To none, we are told, does the word Safety appeal so forcibly as to those who have been rescued from shipwreck. To have been snatched from that peril, from those engulfing waves, from the cold and exhaustion, and agonised effort to hold on and to hope on, from the suspense, and the expectation every moment of being swept away and lost—yes, truly, the shipwrecked have some idea of what it is to be saved, of what it will be to stand upon the Eternal Shore and look back upon the darkness of life's sea, upon the dangers that all but overwhelmed us, the doubts and fears, the clinging of Faith when Hope and Love seemed gone; upon the Hand that was stretched out to us, the word: "It is I," the Presence that rescued and sustained us to the end and brought us where we are.

What will it be to see the doors of Heaven from the inside, and know that by no possibility can the shadow of danger come near us any more, "for the reward of God continueth for ever."[1] To behold across the abyss our enemy the devil, chained, and know that never again will any breath of temptation reach us. To see the world in its true light. How contemptible its principles and its allurements look from this height, yet how insidious we see its influence to be and how formidable its snares! And the flesh, the most dangerous of our three enemies, the treacherous ally that so often sided with the foe and gave us more trouble than the other two together—what of that? Our conflict with it is over, the soul has come triumphant out of the struggle, and the body passing through its purgatory, not indeed of pain but of humiliation unspeakable, wrecked and ruined to all seeming, is safe in His hands who will "reform it and make it like to the body of His glory."[2] Through its frequent union during life with the sacred flesh of its Saviour, through His solemn promise to it in virtue of that union,[3] "my flesh shall rest in hope."[4]

Rest and Peace—the twofold blessing with which, in the beautiful language of her early days, the Church lays us to sleep when life's work is done, the prayer for us which will never cease till she sees the last of the Elect safely Home!

Rest. But the reward of rest supposes labour. If I want the rest of evening I must be able to show the fruits of the day's toil. What am I making ready for that evening when the Master of the vineyard will say: "Call the labourers and pay them their hire"?

I have a twofold task in life, the training of my soul by the correction of the evil in it and the development of

---

1   Ecclus. 18:22.   2   Philip. 3:21.   3   John 6.
4   Ps. 15:9.

the good, in order to bring out in myself the likeness to Christ which will fit me for a place in His Kingdom. And secondly, the work for others which in one shape or another is required of us all. Am I providing this? Negative work, the simple harming of none, will not suffice, even were it possible. Service such as this did not avail the unprofitable servant of the Gospel, and will not avail me or entitle me to rest. "What good shall I do that I may have life everlasting?"[1] "Hate not laborious works ordained by the Most High",[2] is the admonition for this life; "they shall rest from their labour",[3] is the promise for the next. Everyone must labour. "Man is born to labour and the bird to fly."[4] God lays the materials at our door in the shape of talents and opportunities; it is for us to turn them into merit and titles to reward and rest.

Peace. We all know the sensation produced on us by a glorious sunset after a stormy day; when the thunderclouds are rolled away and the western sky is lovely with the delicate tints brought by the rain; when the stillness of the country air is broken only by the quiet sounds of evening, and from freshened leaves and dripping fern rise scents that fill our very soul with fragrance and with ecstasy. What will it be when the storms of passion are lulled for ever; when "the sun shall go down no more, and the days of our mourning shall be ended";[5] and the tears of earth, if their memory remains when the hand of God has wiped them away,[6] will shine only with the glory they reflect!

---

1 Matth. 19:16.   2 Ecclus. 7:16.   3 Apoc. 14:13.
4 Job 5:7.   5 Isaias 60:20.   6 Apoc. 7:17.

We know, too, the sense of relief and gladness with which the heart of a nation beats when, after a long and anxious war, peace is proclaimed. What shall it be when the soul, so long a battlefield, shall be the field of a victory whose fruits shall last for ever; when sword and shield, all "the armour of God" by which in the evil day we were able "to extinguish the fiery darts of the most wicked one,"[1] shall be taken from our weary hands and replaced by the victor's palm! Within and around us God shall proclaim a universal peace—peace with Him, stable throughout eternity, peace with the partners in our eternal joy, peace with ourselves: our faculties at rest because in possession of their object, all working together in perfect harmony, undisturbed both within and without by anything that could trouble for an instant their perfect content and bliss!

The Joy of Memory. What sweetness there will be here, as we recall past crosses, struggles, and victories; past penance that has made joy in Heaven; past service, light and unworthy but so magnificently requited; past grace which has so abundantly blossomed into glory! Sweetness, above all, in the remembrance of God's dealings with our soul—of the Providence that embraced our life from first to last "reaching from end to end mightily and ordering all things sweetly."[2] "As a man traineth up his son, so the Lord thy God hath trained thee up.[3] "The Lord hath carried thee as a man is wont to carry his little son all the way that you have come to this place."[4] "I have been with thee wherever thou hast walked,"[5] and "all thy ways were prepared."[6] Could

---

1 Ephes. 6:16. 2 Wisd. 8:1. 3 Deut. 8:5.
4 Deut. 1:31. 5 2 Kings 7:9. 6 Judith 9:5.

there be any regret in that retrospect, it would come from the memory of those hours when mistrust overshadowed our soul and hid from us the ever mindful, ever tender love of our Father who is in Heaven.

Joy in our Faith of heretofore, when we see the light to which it has brought us, when we know by experience the truth of our Lord's words: "Blessed are they that have not seen and have believed;"[1] when we find mists swept away, difficulties gone, obscurities all lost in the blaze of Truth, in the light of God's Countenance. What joy that we held on to His word and to the hand of His Church and would not be staggered by the whisperings of infidelity or misbelief! "With the hearing of the ear I have heard Thee, but now my eye seeth Thee."[2]

Joy in our Hope, when we see how trust glorified God and is justified in Heaven beyond all measure and desire. "What I do thou knowest not now but thou shalt know hereafter,"[3] He said to us in the day of our trouble long ago. And we believed and hoped—and now to see what He has given us in reward!

Joy most of all in our Charity. "Now there remain Faith, Hope and Charity, these three, but the greatest of these is Charity."[4] Greatest because "it is poured forth in our hearts by the Holy Ghost who is given to us,"[5] and because it is never superseded. Faith and Hope brought us to the gates of Heaven and there took leave of us, for their work was done. But "Charity never falleth away."[6] It alone remains, unalterable through the Eternal Years, for "they shall see

---

1   John 20:29.   2   Job 42:5.   3   John 13:7.
4   1 Cor. 13:13.   5   Rom. 5:5.   6   1 Cor. 13:8.

His Face"[1] and "the loveliness of His beauty,"[2] "the Beloved of the beloved."[3]

What joy there will be in every aspiration of love in time, that has increased our nearness to Him in eternity! What joy, too, in the love we have shown Him in all who were His, when He thanks us for it as shown to Himself: "As long as you did it to one of these My least brethren, you did it to Me."[4]

Joy of the Understanding—flooded with light, satisfied at last with Truth, face to face with mysteries, which remain and must remain such to every finite intelligence, but into which the soul may gaze and gaze, which it may penetrate more and more, with ever growing wonder and delight. "In Thy light we shall see light."[5] "We see through a glass in a dark manner, but then face to face. Now I know in part, but then I shall know even as I am known."[6]

Joy of the Will—the royal power of the soul, having the tremendous responsibility of freedom and of choice. How often, like the quicksilver of the barometer, it has fluctuated during life—what joy now to see it fixed at "Set Fair" for ever, all its choices, desires, affections, absolutely conformed to the Will of God, confirmed in good, in what is best, without the fear of ever swerving again! What joy for us, who have had so much cause to mistrust ourselves and fear for the future, to know that we can never, never again misuse any creature, or fall short of the perfect praise, reverence, and service of God for which we were created, to know that all our joy in any creature, all our happiness

---

1   Apoc. 22:4.   2   Ps. 49:2.   3   Ps. 67:13.
4   St. Matth. 25:40.   5   Ps. 35:10.   6   1 Cor. 13:12.

throughout eternity will be glory and contentment to Him who makes us welcome to all He has and is: "Good and faithful servant, enter thou into the joy of thy Lord!"

Joy in the Gifts of Glory. After the Resurrection we shall receive back from the hand of God the body that was our companion in life, endowed with new and wonderful powers—immortality, impassibility, agility, clarity. It can neither die henceforth nor suffer. It can pass with the rapidity of thought from one point to another, however distant. Like the Body of Christ after His Resurrection, it can penetrate substance. It is glorious with heavenly light, an object of admiration and delight to all the Blessed and to God Himself.

Joy in our Companions. "There the wicked cease from troubling and the weary are at rest."[1] "There no one shall resist thee, no man shall complain of thee, no man shall hinder thee, nothing shall stand in thy way."[2] All around are friends, bound to us by ties closer than any known on earth. Those we have helped in life, those who have helped us, how they long for our company; what joy, what congratulations there will be when we arrive amongst them! Think of being welcomed and acknowledged as one of that glorious family "where all shall be called and shall be the sons of God"[3]—Confessors and Virgins, Martyrs and Apostles, Angels and Archangels, all looking upon us as brothers and sisters, the Queen of Heaven herself owning us as dearly loved servants and children! Think of mingling with them on terms of equality, not feeling

---

1   Job 3:17.

2   *Imit.*, Bk. 3, ch. 49   3   1 John 3:1.

awkward, not out of place, but worthy of them, at home with them from the first!

The Reunions of Heaven. But who shall tell the joy when those to whom we were bound on earth by ties of friendship or kindred, come forth from the bright ranks to welcome us and claim us as their own! When we recognise them amid all that glory as the same; when we find again the love of bygone days, purified, perfected, yet the same that was our joy on earth; when we go over with them God's dealings with us in the past, in the changes and trials of life, and see and own with thanksgiving and praise: "He hath done all things well!"

The blessedness of this reunion with those we love, loses with some its power of consolation by perplexing questions and mistaken notions as to our life in Heaven. "Will God so absorb every faculty of our souls as to make them indifferent to all beside? Are the ties of earth's relationships broken for ever by the hand of Death, or will they be reformed in Heaven to exist throughout eternity? Shall we know our own there and love and be loved as in the old days here?"

Holy Scripture seems itself to answer these questions for us. In the intercourse of our Lord with His friends after His Resurrection do we note any diminution of His affection for them, any ignoring of former ties, any forgetfulness? Or do we find Him on the contrary more mindful, more tender than before?

We do indeed note one difference, one that appeals with singular force to our human hearts and experience. There is a playfulness about His dealings with them in

His Risen Life that is one of its special and most attractive features. The baptism with which He had to be baptised, that lay like a weight upon His Soul all life through—was over, and a joyousness, unseen before, appears in Him. He hides from Mary Magdalen, watches her as she seeks Him, questions her about her trouble and her tears, hears her loving plans, and at last, for the consolation of His own Heart as much as for hers, reveals Himself, calling her by her name. He walks between two of His disciples during an afternoon, hidden from their eyes but making their hearts burn within them, and when His work for them is done, makes Himself known to them—and disappears.

He comes in sweet surprises when the Eleven are met together, not for prayer but for the evening meal—a more homely hour, better suited to their needs and His designs. At a time when intercourse between friends is freest, He could better, by reviving old memories and courtesies, and by acts of condescension, so tender as to seem hardly consistent with His glorified state, reassure them as to His identity; that it was indeed "Jesus yesterday, today, and the same for ever"[1], who came and went, and taught, and chid, and comforted as before. "It is I, fear not....Why are you troubled, and why do thoughts arise in your hearts?" They think Him a spirit—and He shows them His hands and feet, and eats before them the honeycomb put tremblingly into His hands. They think that even should it be Himself, He must be different now, different at least to them who have shown themselves such sorry friends

---

1   Heb. 13:8.

in need—and He calls them by the new and endearing name of "brethren." "See My hands and My feet that it is I Myself, handle Me and see." He repeats, He insists, He omits nothing to convince them that His glorious life which has changed so much, has left His love for them the same. He blesses their fruitless fishing with a miraculous draught as in the past. He invites them to dine, prepares their meal, and "passing, ministers to them," the words by which He Himself describes His gracious familiarity with His servants in the future Kingdom of God.[1]

Speaking of the General Resurrection, St. John says: "We are now the sons of God, and it hath not yet appeared what we shall be. We know that when He shall appear we shall be like to Him because we shall see Him as He is."[2]

Like Him. How affectionate, then, how anxious for reunion with those who have sorrowed on our account, how desirous to show ourselves still the same: "Behold and see that it is I Myself." It will be the old love purified and perfected, but tender as ever. What was beautiful in the relations of earth will be preserved in Heaven, that only having passed away which is inconsistent with the state of glory. In that Holy Family which is the model of all others, the Son of God will still and for ever be the Son of Mary, and Joseph's Foster Son. How, then, can we doubt that the exceeding joy resulting from reunion with those dear to us here, is reserved for us hereafter! In her prayer for father and mother, the Church puts these words on our lips: "Grant that I may see them again in eternal glory."

1 Luke 12:37.   2   1 John 3:2.

But if there are some who refuse themselves the consolation of these thoughts, there are others who seem to look forward to these sweet reunions as to the main happiness of Heaven. This is, of course, to misconceive utterly the nature of that happiness. They are but one of its joys, thrown as it were into the scale to make it overflow, no more to be compared with the essential and supreme joy of the Vision of God than the thin fringe of surf can be compared with the ocean. But it helps us to realise something of Heaven's beatitude, something of God's liberality, something of the promise: "they shall be inebriated with the plenty of Thy house, Thou shalt make them drink of the torrent of Thy pleasure,"[1] that the joy they will bring should be an accessory merely, but one of God's rewards, over and above the "reward exceeding great"[2] which is Himself.

Joy in our God. Here we are out of our depth at once, carried away and lost in an ocean without sounding or shore. What will it be to have reached the End for which we were created, to enter upon the true life for which life on earth was but preparation and probation; to live at each moment the fullest, most intense life of which the powers of our soul, quickened and strengthened beyond conception, are henceforth capable; to be able to employ upon God with their whole energy, easily, delightedly, perpetually, the faculties which on earth were so hard to fix; no tension, no fatigue; unceasing activity coupled with absolute repose; content without satiety; the discovery in Him of new marvels, new beauties, with delight in the

---

1 Ps. 35:9.   2 Gen. 15:1.

discovery ever fresh, ever new—and this throughout eternity!

> It may not be,
> That one who looks upon that light, can turn
> To other object, willingly, his view.
> For all the good that will may covet, there
> Is summ'd; and all, elsewhere defective found
> Complete.[1]

"Enter into the joy of thy Lord!" O sweetest of invitations! to enter in and take possession of Him in whom is all good, all we can desire—Holiness, Beauty, Tenderness, Wisdom and Strength and Joy at the Fountain head. To see all things in Him, and love all with and in Him; to have Him as our own possession without fear of ever losing Him; to cry out to Him with the Blessed Curé d'Ars: "My God, I have Thee at last, I hold Thee fast, Thou shalt never escape me any more!"

The happiness of the Blessed overflows on every side. The cup of each is full, and, for the love they bear one another, the joy of each is the joy of all. "Alleluia shall be sung in its streets,"[2] is said of the Heavenly City, and truly such song must be a necessity for those full hearts. "God is attended by ten thousand, thousands of them that rejoice."[3] "And they shall be His people, and God Himself with them shall be their God. And God shall wipe away all tears from their eyes, and death shall be no more, nor mourning, nor crying, nor sorrow shall be any more, for the former things are passed away.... And they shall see His Face, and His

---

1　*Paradise*, Canto XXXII, Dante.
2　Tobias 13:22.　　　　　3　Ps. 67:18.

name shall be on their foreheads... and they shall reign for ever and ever."[1]

This is what waits for us: a few years at most, and all this will be ours! Can we wonder that the Church, whose mission it is to soothe the sorrows of Time by the hope of Eternity, is always seeking to lift our hearts above the trials and losses of earth to the treasure we have in Heaven, that her daily cry to us from ten thousand altars is

"Sursum Corda!"

---

1   Apoc. 21:3-4, 22:4-5.

Additional titles available from

St. Augustine Academy Press
Books for the Traditional Catholic

Titles by Mother Mary Loyola:

Blessed are they that Mourn
Confession and Communion
Coram Sanctissimo (Before the Most Holy)
First Communion
First Confession
Forgive us our Trespasses
Hail! Full of Grace
Heavenwards
Holy Mass/How to Help the Sick and Dying
Home for Good
Jesus of Nazareth: The Story of His Life Written for Children
Questions on First Communion
The Child of God: What comes of our Baptism
The Children's Charter
The Little Children's Prayer Book
The Soldier of Christ: Talks before Confirmation
Trust
Welcome! Holy Communion Before and After

Titles by Father Lasance:

The Catholic Girl's Guide
The Young Man's Guide

Tales of the Saints:

A Child's Book of Saints by William Canton
A Child's Book of Warriors by William Canton
Legends & Stories of Italy by Amy Steedman
Mary, Help of Christians by Rev. Bonaventure Hammer
Page, Esquire and Knight by Marion Florence Lansing
The Book of Saints and Heroes by Leonora Lang
Saint Patrick: Apostle of Ireland
The Story of St. Elizabeth of Hungary by William Canton

Check our Website for more:

www.staugustineacademypress.com

www.ingramcontent.com/pod-product-compliance
Lightning Source LLC
Chambersburg PA
CBHW031830090426

42741CB00005B/194